GARDENING

A WINDOW ON OUR SOUL

Kathleen P. O'Beirne
Lifescape Enterprises

Other Books by the Author:

Life Is a Beach: Musings from the Sea

Birds of a Feather: Lessons from the Sea

> *Birds of a Feather: Behavior Patterns Matrix*
> *Birds of a Feather: Educator's Guide*
> *Birds of a Feather: Parent's Guide*

Mindscapes & Mindsets

Copyright © 2012 by Kathleen P. O'Beirne
First Edition: June 2012

Published by:
Lifescape Enterprises
P. O. Box 218
West Mystic, CT 06388

Library of Congress Number: 2012903998
ISBN 978-1-879979-05-5

10 9 8 7 6 5 4 3 2 1
Graphic Designer: Jeanne Sigel
Architectural Perspectivist: Michael P. O'Beirne

Cover Photograph: Dana Jensen, *The Day*
Author's Photograph: Jeff Evans, *The Day*
Printed by *The Day Printing Company*, New London, CT

Dedication

for all those who have had
the vision, energy, and persistence
to cultivate gardens
(both botanical and metaphorical)

May your foresight, toil, and delight
infuse us all
for generations to come.

May your discoveries
be both scientific
(helping to diminish the effects of cancer)
and aesthetic
(helping our souls to soar).

Of Soil and Soul

One of my favorite hymns has been buzzing in my brain as I have worked on this book – "I come to the garden alone, while the dew is still on the roses... " A favorite even when I was a little girl, this hymn was sung without questioning. But lately, I noticed the final lines in verse one: "And the joys we share as we tarry there, none other has ever known."

Quite to the contrary, I believe that many experience their higher selves, their joys, peace, and visions while gardening. It ranks on the top of Abraham Maslow's "Hierarchy of Needs" — the realm of the philosophical or religious. True, it has been a source of food, one of Maslow's basic levels of human needs; but it has been the inspiration of poets, artists, and religious writers from the early centuries on.

This book is subtitled *A Window on Our Soul*, because I see this as a collaborative endeavor. Readers and I together explore the messages, mysteries, and metaphors found in our gardening experiences. Even though I address you, the reader, as "you," you will know that I am sharing our potential communal insights.

I heard recently from a dear friend that she had a neighbor who was offended that she went into the neighbor's garden while she was hard at work. Ruffled, she said, "This is my quiet time. Please call me and make an appointment before you come over." Obviously, this is fairly far along the privacy continuum. Others see gardening as a much more social endeavor, relishing time spent working as a team refurbishing downtown planters.

Where do you fall on this continuum?

Your answer may be situational. When you have planned for a team or solo stint, you may not want the parameters changed.

As gardening is the number one hobby in America, there must be nourishment of all sorts going on. This book is designed to help you tease out the richnesses in your horticultural endeavors.

I think that it is important to stress that my gardens are Everyman's Gardens – they have been planted a little bit at a time, as energy and acquisition permitted. They are not the result of a grand plan, nor a landscaper's equipment. They are the result of friends' gifts, library and church fair specimens, and purchases through catalogs and local nurseries.

The seasonal metaphor of our life is always in the back of my mind; but I have resisted ordering the contents of this book on that pattern. The first chapter focuses on the ways in which our lives mimic the seasons and gets that compelling parallel out of the way so that we can explore other themes that I hope you will find even more intriguing. That will rob you of the comfort of moving sequentially through the year but, hopefully, the juxtapositions of seasons may help you notice how the over-arching themes carry throughout the year and throughout our lives. Even though one might expect more challenges, the chapters clearly show that delights and insights reign.

My current reality encompasses two gardens. One in downtown Mystic, CT, with a 1926 Dutch Colonial. The second is a pond-front site with glacial remains and a 1930's farmhouse in Ledyard, CT. For more on other gardens that I have known and loved, please see the white pages at the end of the book, which contain the landscape plans (generalized) for my Mystic and Long Pond acres, as well as an index that lists the common names first, with the Latin in parentheses. I have chosen the non-traditional approach of capitalizing flowers, trees, and creatures in order to give them importance.

Now, sit back, read slowly, ponder, and observe...

My gratitude to my three soil-and-soul mates:

My husband, Mick O'Beirne, my companion in gardening and life, whose creative fixes for all of my "neat ideas" have been much appreciated.

Jeanne Sigel, the gifted graphic designer for this book, whose sensitive selections of fonts and illustrations have made it a botanic feast.

And Michael P. O'Beirne, my architect son, whose renderings of our gardens give you a Pooh Bear map to help you visualize our plantings.

Thanks also to advance reader Patricia Schaefer, who provided helpful insights.

Kathleen P. O'Beirne

Contents

Prologue: Of Soil and Soul i

Contents iii

How to Use This Book xv

I Lifescaping.... 1

    Lifescaping 3
    Name Tags 4
    Windows on Our Garden World 5
    Solitude Feeds the Soul 6
    A Formula for Health 7
    Every Day a New Wave of Color 8
    A Lesson from Johnny Appleseed 9
    Greenhouses 10
    Waning Days of Summer 12
    Continue Watering Well Into Fall 13
    Critical Fall Chores 14
    Little Orange Balls of Delight 15
    Autumn Through Rose-Colored Glasses 16
    Keeping Gardens Attractive in Autumn 17
    Precious Few 18
    Expectations 19
    Harbingers of Fall 20
    Razzle-Dazzle 21
    Scraggly Fall 23
    End-of-Season Chives 24
    The Leaves are Falling 26
    Parting is Such Sweet Sorrow 27
    Harvest Moon 28
    Winter Sunsets 29
    Inspiration from Our Winter Garden 30
    Invincible Summer 31
    Gardening is Not for the Faint of Heart 32
    Winter is Not for Wimps 33
    Pods in Winter 34
    What to Winter-Over? 35

II Design 37

Finding the Place Just Right 39
Size and Scope 40
Nature or Nurture? 41
Placement = Art + Science 42
Exposure 43
Garden Gates 44
Garden Benches 46
Lights in the Garden 47
Sculpture in the Garden 48
Green Fences 50
Creative Collaboration 51
Wind in the Willows 52
More Than the Sum of Their Parts 53
Random by Design 54
There are Times to Plan 56
Gardens in Moonlight 57
A Bulbilicious Day 58
Butterfly Choreography 59
Incubation 60
Nursery Purchases – Sinful Expenditures? 61
Burgundy Accents 62
Happy Flowers 63
Extraordinaires 64
Exclamation Points 65
Supplemental Color 66
Craving Pink 67
Of Birds and Berries 68
Hawthorn Heaven 69

III **Maintenance**... 71

Planting and Maintenance.............................. 73
Priorities... 74
Gloves... 75
Spring Muscles.. 76
Soggy Soil... 77
Mulch... 78
Making Supports Invisible.............................. 79
Nutrients... 80
Manure.. 81
Bulb Food.. 82
Hose Guides.. 83
Untidiness... 84
Thinning vs. Pruning...................................... 85
Patience and Perseverance = P^2.................... 86
Tiger Lilies.. 87
Resolutions... 88
Pachysandra: Pride or Prejudice?.................. 90
Raking Leaves... 91
Waste Not... 92
Our Public Face.. 93
Gardening as a Cumulative Experience.......... 94
Almost Maintenance-Free.............................. 95
Less Is More.. 96
Debris from the Garden................................. 97
Clean Up as You Go Along............................. 98
It is a Work in Progress................................. 99
One Size Fits All... 100
Cleaning Out the Potting Sheds.................... 101
The Good Enough Garden............................. 102

IV   Acquisition... 103

    Spring Pink Fireworks 105
    Reaping What We Sow 106
    Lunaria Lust 107
    End of Summer "Pow" 108
    Beautyberry 109
    Annual vs. Hardy Tulip Bulbs 110
    Garden Bags and Pots 111
    One Woman's Excess = Another's Treasure 112
    Vessels 113
    Winterberries vs. Sparkleberries 114
    Self-Sowers 115
    Seeds and Rootings 116
    Locaflor 118
    Friendship Gardens 119
    Fashion and Flowers 120

V   Tools.. 121

    Tool Bag vs. Tool Box 123
    Tools of My Dreams 124
    Awesome Auger 128
    All I Want for Christmas 129
    Aprons as Armor 130
    Disinfect Your Tools, Containers, and Gloves 131
    Function-Discrete Areas 132

VI Challenges 133

    What Grows Here? 135
    Who's Been In My Yard? 137
    No Man Is an Island 138
    Transplanting 139
    Don't Move Once Established 140
    Weeds – Random Acts of Unkindness 141
    Tenacity – a Weed's Middle Name 142
    Early Spring Pestilents 144
    Foolish Mistake 145
    Jumping Junipers! 146
    Things That Go Hop in Your Garden 147
    Sweet Woodruff 148
    The Dichotomy of Acorns 149
    Too Much of a Good Thing 150
    Rain 151
    Hurricane Debris 152
    Over-Exposure 153
    Snow Casts 154
    Crisis Management 155
    The Climate is Changing 156
    Location³ 157
    Drought Indicators 158
    Poisonous Beauties 159
    Bumps, Bruises, and Bites 160
    Crabgrass 161
    Weeding = Time for Meditation 162
    Lemonade 163
    Sharing a Garden is Hard to Do! 164
    Gardens: For Ourselves? For Others? 165
    Voices on the Pond 166

VII Delights... 167

    Little Delights 169
    Beguiling Witch Hazel 170
    Little Blue Scillas 171
    Garden Tours with a Friend 172
    Can You Find? 173
    They Can Live to be 100! 174
    Fernaholics 175
    Begonias 176
    Scentsational 177
    Aroma therapy – Au Naturel 178
    Citronella Candles 179
    The Vegetable Dog 180
    Lightning Bugs and Stars 181
    Monarch of All I Survey 182
    Surprise Lilies 183
    Recipes for Herbal Profusion 184
    Mozart Chutney 186
    Cloudy Skies 187
    Dancing Grasses 188
    Magical Garden Sounds 189
    Pond Presents 190

VIII Insights 191

S^3 – Sustainable, Sustained, and Sustaining 193
Awareness and Awe 194
Arise and Greet the Day 195
Tansy Lesson 196
Quarks for Quirky People 197
Pockets of Rockets 198
Buying Bulbs – Investment Lesson 199
Sharing Your Passion 201
Deadheading and Pinching Back 202
Sum and Substance 203
Lady's Slippers = Mid-Life Crisis 204
Irrational Exuberance 205
How Do the Birds Know? 206
Moveable Feasts 207
Flower Arranging 208
Quasi-Harbingers 209
Reflections = V^3 210
Roots 211
It's Sunset – Do You Know Where Your Pelican Is? . 212
Hope Springs Eternal 213
Life's Kindling 214
What is so Rare? 215
Ah and Awe 216
Gratitude is an Attitude 217
Late Bloomers 218
The Anniversary Japanese Maple 219
Multi-tasking 220

VIII Insights...*Cont'd*

       Five Miles Per Hour 221

       Some Crave Crowds 222

       Fiddleheads – Truth Unfolding 223

       Portable Pots 224

       Don't Tread on Fragile Ground......................... 225

       Give a Garden Party 226

       Sheds 227

       Strange Bedfellows... 228

       I Saved a Swallowtail Butterfly Today 229

       Garden Clubs 230

       Planting Forward 231

       Peek Experiences 232

       Ivy Wreathes the Pines 234

       Directed Dreaming... 235

       Weary, Dirty, and Satisfied 236

       Winter of My Content 237

       Lights in the Snow 238

       The Fruits of Our Labors................................... 239

       Epilogue 240

IX   Index.. 241

X   Bibliography 245

XI   O'Beirne Garden Drawings 246

XII Gardens I Have Known and Loved 251

      Author's Biography 252

XIII Re-order Information 253

How to Use This Book

I suggest reading this book in small portions, just as it was written, allowing time to muse and mull on the implications for your own life. There are enough sections to savor several a week for the seasons in which you cannot be in your garden on a daily basis, or to read when your physical labors are done.

Another option is to take it with you when you are traveling and have blocks of time to ponder. Dog-ear the ones you like best and want to revisit. You may choose to use some of the metaphors for workshops or retreats – they are designed for either personal or group reflections.

As you muse, query at least three domains:

Your gardens themselves.

Your personal or family life.

Your income-producing domain (which many call "work" or "job") and your volunteer connections (perhaps your real work).

All three domains can benefit from a new angle of vision. Consistency in your approach across all three domains strengthens your likelihood of using new strategies productively.

I hope that you will engage in participatory reading – marking your comments in the margins. You could even use a different color of pen each time you revisit. My copy of Anne Morrow Lindbergh's *Gift from the Sea* is a colorful record of how my insights have changed over time. The exciting thing is that she has new messages for me every time I read her book.

Metaphors enable us to see with "new eyes" – a talent to be cherished. We are new each day of our lives, so need new eyes to see new truths. The scrim pages of this book feature Fiddleheads, my metaphor for truth unfolding...

LIFESCAPING...

Lifescaping

In 1981, while developing a series of articles for *Family Magazine* on volunteering and keeping a balance in our lives, I hit upon the concept of lifescaping. It has served me well personally and I have shared it with many others through workshops and articles. We can approach our life's design in much the same way as we do our landscapes, noting which ingredients should be perennials and which could be showy annuals.

There are two basic styles of landscaping with many variations along the continuum. There is the carefully planned garden or yard, with consideration of soil, temperature, topography, and seasons. At the other extreme is the opportunistic version that incorporates whatever the gardener likes, receives as gifts, and sees in others' designs. We often live our lives following one of these patterns.

One of the primary theses of lifescaping is that we should each <u>choose</u> our own <u>creative balance</u>. And, we should feel empowered when others attempt to thrust responsibilities upon us to say, "Thank you for thinking of me, but it does not fit my creative balance at this time." People are usually stunned by the audacity of the concept! You have said it with a smile, but have been firm.

How would having a lifescape in mind serve you well?

When could you have used such a plan in the past?

Remember that like all plans, it should be flexible in order to accommodate unforeseen opportunities.

You are not required to make your plan public! Like your Myers-Briggs Type Indicator (personality profile), this is personal information to inform your own decisions vs. being used by others to manipulate you.

3

Nametags

"It looks like you're growing nametags!" quipped a dear friend and sister seeker of metaphors. When I looked at my pond beds through her eyes, I saw the endless plastic and metal tags I had so carefully installed to help me remember the new names (and not over-plant the next year before determining if they had survived). Because she was absolutely right and funny to boot, I was not offended.

My college arboretum and botanical gardens are rife with nametags (which alumnae copy copiously at reunions), so I did not see my proliferation of plant identifications from the aesthetic viewpoint... just the scientific.

In order not to clutter these pages with nametags, I will list the referenced species in the Index under their common names (with their botanical names in parentheses). This should satisfy both our aesthetic and scientific tastes.

How could I better ensure my ability to identify what I have planted? I must find a more aesthetic way to trigger my memory. Perhaps an erasable pad to scale would allow me to note the newcomers.

Such a strategy would also work for my ever-changing neighbors (with their address and phone number added).

What other areas of our life could use a chart with an erasable surface?

Are there areas in which our record keeping is excessive? For example, household expenditures?

Windows on
Our Garden World

Through the years I have been blessed with windows I visited daily to give me a read on the day. In our home in Arlington, Virginia, our master bathroom window overlooked the Oak tree canopy of our ridge – hence, our Oak Ridge place name. It was full of Crows, Squirrels, and Chipmunks. When a major storm was brewing, we could see the trees torquing as the wind blew up the street at right angles behind us and then hit the canopy.

From my original bath window on Long Pond, Connecticut, I could see Ferns, Pipsissewa, and Moss – and smell them, too, in warm weather. They were on a shady bank beside the one-story cabin and our awning-style window could be left open in most weather.

For many of us, the kitchen sink window gets lots of use. What have you planted or placed in that vista? In Mystic, my Redbud is glorious from there. I can see the Goldfinches visiting our cutting garden seedpods and the birdbath. The Cardinals and Chickadees visit in all seasons, and the whole bird world descends upon the Winterberries in late January or early February, depending on the daily temperatures and snowfall.

From my home office window overlooking Route 1 in Mystic, I see a Hawthorn in bloom, Crabapples a cloud of pink, and Smoke Trees adding their burgundy accent in late spring. As I work at dusk in mid-winter, I can see the sun going down through the silhouetted trees. Enjoy your windows on the world.

Where do you look carefully at your world?

Do you see your landscape plan with new eyes and plan the next trimming? Planting?

Do you marvel at the maturing composition in your view?

Do you take time to look at your life the same way?

Solitude Feeds the Soul

"The gardener does not love to talk," said Robert Louis Stevenson in his poem, *The Gardener*. Gardening for me is a quiet pursuit, a reverie – while the hands and back work, the mind goes elsewhere, following its own bidding. Akin to prayer and meditation, this mental state flowers best without conscious attention.

Andrew Marvell (1620 – 78) in his poem, *The Garden*, took the next leap:

> *Here at the fountain's sliding foot,*
> *Or at some fruit-tree's mossy root,*
> *Casting the body's vest aside,*
> *My soul into the boughs does glide:*
> *There, like a bird, it sits and sings,*
> *Then whets and combs its silver wings,*
> *And, till prepared for longer flight,*
> *Waves in its plumes the various light.*

Have you had similar experiences in your garden?

How can you lay the groundwork for continued soul flights?

Do they come when sought or do they creep in unbidden?

6

A Formula for Health

Surprise, surprise… a recent update on a 90-year study originated by Dr. Lewis Terman at Stanford University in 1921, concludes that those who garden, walk the dog, and do other active exercise throughout our lives live longest. The pattern of engagement with work and play adds to our longevity, not to mention our delight. Another aspect of gardening plays into a second life-booster, and that is conscientiousness, exemplified by prudence, persistence, and organization.

Those of us who are "driven by dirt," probably already sensed that truth; but now science says it is so. *The Longevity Project* (2011), by researchers Howard Friedman, Ph.D. and Leslie Martin, Ph.D., explains that the pursuit of goals, plus one's detail-orientation and dependability are better predictors than the "eat, drink, and be merry" philosophy.

When did you first begin gardening? Why?

Have there been periods in your life when gardening was put on the back burner? Were there noticeable differences in your quality of life?

Are there periods in each year when you spend less time gardening? What activity do you substitute?

What would be your explanation for gardening's positive effect?

Every Day a New Wave of Color

As on a beach, every day brings a new combination of foliage and blooms in the garden. Even though today may be similar to yesterday, there are subtle changes in the hues, the number of blossoms, and the textures. When we are attuned to these incremental variations, we can be excited by each new day. We can take pleasure in the bud, the early bloom, and the later bloom, each with its own migrating color tone. And the seed pods are yet to come.

How like our lives this is. In families and other relationships, every day is a new day. New relationships bring certain anticipatory emotions. Developing relationships bring some knowns and unknowns. Our children certainly provide us with new selves daily (if not hourly, by adolescence). And we mirror their growing patterns with some sensitivities of our own – opportunities to reflect.... At the other end of the spectrum, we also learn from the dying stalks. What has been so beautiful now must reside in our memories.

Those who believe in God's grace see each day as an opportunity to begin anew to be what God would hope we could be. What an extravagant gift – to carry the best forward, trim back what is no longer useful or attractive, and honor its former beauty.

Do you purposely build in a sequence of blooms and foliage?

Many of us have belatedly learned that secret by planting compatible perennials as the seasons go by. Or conversely, removing less desirable clumps in crowded seasons.

Do you value the variety playing out before you?

8

A Lesson from Johnny Appleseed

My mother literally planted an Apple tree in the yard of each house we lived in, whether the yards were in Army housing or houses that Mom and Dad owned. She loved making applesauce and would mix Crabapples and regular Apples for jelly – often for the Army wives' club bazaar.

My focus has been less culinary. I was interested in having Hollies and, hopefully, berries for holiday wreaths and bouquets. In Mystic, soon after we bought the house, we planted native Alders (deciduous Hollies from a friend's "back forty") and Inkberry bushes, plus various Ilex species with small leaves and inauspicious berries.

When we moved to Arlington, Virginia, for Pentagon duty, we planted Nellie Stevens Hollies in a backyard corner. Their free-form rapid growth and beautiful big berries kept us well supplied for the holidays. A more traditional, pyramidal Holly was planted at the end of the sun porch to screen the air conditioner and garbage cans.

When we returned to Mystic upon retirement, we added an American Holly (which has never been really robust), Blue Prince Hollies (pretty in the yard, but the leaves quickly turn black in arrangements), yellow-berried Hollies, and variegated Hollies. One of our favorites, Winterberry, is deciduous and has absolutely fabulous berries. Its self-pollinating look-alike, Sparkleberry, has fewer berries, but the birds love them. We have planted for the winter season, not only in our yards, but also in our lives.

What evergreen species have you planted?

What evergreen interests/passions have you nurtured for your life?

What evergreen projects/programs have you initiated for those who follow?

Greenhouses

The greenhouse holds an almost mythic space in my mind – the place where the exceedingly wealthy or bona fide botanists can work on the "fountain of youth." They can cheat the seasons by starting new plants well ahead of when they would be suitably planted outside, or they can maintain wonderful specimens that would not survive the prevailing climate (hot or cold, humid or dry). Their architecture often replicates castle-like motifs, with walls of glass instead of stone. They are a magical domain – truly out of the ordinary.

They are places where those who inhabit them explore a passionate interest. It may be a business interest that requires a specially manipulated environment, like a nursery or a bio-medical startup. Incubators for small businesses mimic this concept – the "plants" are too young and too fragile to be planted in an unpredictable climate. They must grow strong first and then withstand the transplanting to the real world.

Children are much like this – hence, the term "nursery."
I think that most of us believe that they deserve early nurturance,
an opportunity to sprout their wings, and discover their
unique characteristics.

*How have you "hardened" plants? Do you have a
greenhouse? Have you longed for one? What stops you?*

*Do you know gardeners who have or have had
greenhouses? What is their assessment? Have they used
them once the novelty wore off?*

*In our area, one of the state park properties includes a
greenhouse under rehabilitation (with substantial fund-
raising required for this on-going project). What is the real
appeal (vs. the historic restoration logic)?*

*Long-term, can we afford plants/interests/investments that
cannot thrive in our climate? Are they worth the
greenhouse investment?*

*Could hydroponic processes provide food
that our planet desperately needs without the
soil component?*

At what cost?

Waning Days of Summer

"Got to take advantage of the good days," said a mid-life female kayaker who visits our pond in the summer and early fall. As she headed out at 5:00 p.m. in her chartreuse kayak, the lowering sun made her luminescent against the still water with reflections of the just-turning trees. My husband and I were sitting on the front porch and I raised my glass of wine as a toast to her sense that time was fleeting. Recognition of the shorter days, less warmth, and the work ethic of fall lurks behind this simple encounter.

We know that we have less time to work in the yard on a daily basis, and yet the tasks of autumn are multiplying: cutting back our perennials and annuals, planting bulbs, raking leaves, and disposing of all of the limbs blown down. The cleanup chores are mixed with the preparation for next spring's glory. The bulbs represent the future; the other debris, the past. And the present... the kayaker.

What special pleasures come with this time of year in your garden? In your life?

As you begin to think about retiring (maybe only for the first time), what similarities do you see in phenomenon of "the waning days?" Do you have bulbs ready to plant? And have you planted some long ago that are reliable bloomers every year?

How do we approach Labor Day weekend? Or even Indian Summer? How much power does the calendar exert over our lives? Our psyches?

Continue Watering Well Into Fall

Many people fail to realize how important it is to keep the soil moist well into autumn. It can be a particularly dry bridge of two seasons and can stress everything from annuals and perennials to significant deciduous and evergreen shrubs. If stressed at this point, they are less equipped to weather the winter. Ground covers are especially sensitive.

Some years ago we had such a fall, with folks losing big old Rhododendrons, Mountain Laurels, Azaleas, and other broad-leafed evergreens. Our Pachysandra and Myrtle (Periwinkle) needed extensive watering to preserve the significant beds that have matured over the years since my early plantings. Recently planted young trees need help at this season as well, such as deciduous Star Magnolias and Witch Hazels.

This is true in our own lives. We should continue to feed our skills and interests as we bridge from our middle to later years. Do our newly launched children need sustenance through some dry seasons?

What are the big shrubs you should nourish (in your landscape and lifescape)?

What are your baseline ground covers?

What perennials or biennials need TLC (tender loving care) at this point?

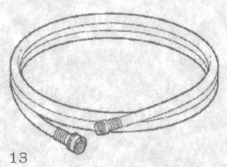

Critical Fall Chores

There is a temptation when the leaves just begin to fall and the garden becomes dry, to cease watering and weeding. Most of the showy blossoms are done, and we are left to tend the few that remain. But, this is a huge mistake. Watering helps the perennial roots stay strong for spring. Weeding avoids the noxious seeds that will make spring a mess. This fall maintenance, which also includes removal of dead stalks and leaves, requires discipline and the vision of seasons ahead.

How like our lives! It is easy to forget the maintenance chores when our flashy projects (perennial or one-time species) have been completed. But, post-florescence is exactly the time to take stock of what went well and what should not be repeated. And, it is the perfect time to nourish the relationships that made your project successful – by thank you notes and by plans for next year.

> *What projects/events do you participate in that mirror this phenomenon?*
>
> *How do weeding, watering, and assessment of this year's garden/life projects help you prepare personally for next year?*
>
> *Which annuals are worth repeating next year? Which are not?*
>
> *Even further out, how do autumn chores prepare us for our metaphorical winter?*

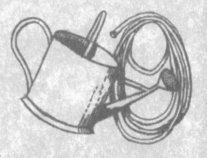

Little Orange Balls of Delight

In early September, the pond terraces are aglow with lots of little orange balls. Some are one to a stem, and other stems have a cluster of four or five balls. Yes, they are Lilies of the Valley in their fall foliage. Can you imagine the delight in the eyes of Chipmunks and Squirrels as they spy these colorful treasures? Acorns are their long-term staple, but these fruits will make luscious living for a couple of weeks. And I will benefit with a new crop of Lilies of the Valley wherever they deposit the seeds.

What are the equivalents in our lives?

What are the short-term, showy fruits of a life that has already provided lovely little blossoms in the spring?

Does grand-parenting or mentoring follow this pattern?

How do the metaphorical seeds spread?

Have you ever heard years later how much something you did impacted someone else? I think these belated recognitions are like these frequently forgotten fruits.

Autumn Through Rose-Colored Glasses

On this gorgeous mid-October day, my husband and I put our kayaks into the pond and I grabbed my red-lensed glasses. They are an old non-prescription pair that I could afford to dunk in the water if some mishap were to befall.

However, they brought an incredible enhancement to my view of the autumn foliage. Making the Swamp Maple leaves even redder, and illuminating the golds of the Sassafras trees, they allowed me to paddle in a sun-dappled world, inhabited only by a pair of Swans, a Great Blue Heron, an Osprey, Mallards, and Turtles warming their shiny shells on pond-edge branches. The Dogwoods' leaves and berries, Burning Bushes, Poison-Ivy vines encircling the trees, and the cherry-sized seeds of the Chinese Dogwoods all exploded with color under the influence of my rose-colored glasses. Our attitude can give equal color to our experiences.

When do you remember your attitude enhancing an actual event?

When did your attitude enhance the memory of an event?

Optimism and the expectation of success often enable us to risk and do remarkable things. When have you had this experience?

As we experience the autumn of our lives, how can our perspective enhance our reality? Our physical and emotional well-being?

Add to your shopping list: a pair of rose-colored glasses. Red rims are spunky, too!

Keeping Gardens Attractive in Autumn

Obviously, it helps if you have planted perennials that bloom in autumn, or at least their foliage turns interesting colors. Evening Primrose leaves turn a brilliant red to offset their dull brown seedpods. Chinese Dogwoods and Mountain Ash bring spectacular berries in autumn. The late bloomers and/or berried bushes and trees may not have been particularly handsome in earlier seasons, so there is a trade-off. Monkshood, which takes up a lot of tall space in my garden until October, comes into its deep purple glory when there is little else still blooming.

If we have not planned ahead, another option is to dig in plants that are in full bloom in autumn, such as Chrysanthemums, Sedums, and Asters. Because they are being transplanted when they are exerting great effort to bloom, they may not survive as perennials. Perhaps their one season of glory is sufficient.

The same challenges occur in the autumn of our lives.

Have you planted skills, abilities, and interests that can come to fruition later in your life? Or, at least continue to be useful to others and a source of delight for you?

Can you add some short-term commitments or projects that would give a special boost to your lifescape?

Could you become a consultant or mentor, bringing spectacular berries as a second career?

Precious Few

The proverbial "last Rose of summer" is indeed a phenomenon that we experience not only as the summer wanes, but as our lives enter a new stage in which blossoms are more rare and, therefore, more treasured.

Just as we trim off the damaged and diseased Hosta leaves so that those remaining can be seen more clearly, we begin to clear out damaged, unused, unattractive items in our life. Books, projects, and possessions that no longer intrigue us are delivered to local book and tag sales. Relationships that no longer fulfill us are set aside. The clutter seems to have ominous weight from which we desire relief.

We have an urge to spend what we now recognize as limited time on earth in ways that are more meaningful to us. We want to "stop and smell the Roses" and cherish the experience. We are less inclined to do things out of habit. Because our energies must be invested carefully, we are more intentional about our choices.

What garden cleaning and life cleaning tasks do you have ahead?

What are your treasured achievements and commitments in which you want to continue to be involved?

What are the activities and practices from which you seek relief?

Are there relationships you wish to sever?
Relationships to grow?

Expectations

In the Bulb There is a Flower – verse 1:
In the cold and snow of winter, there's a spring
that waits to be...
(Hymn 638, Chalice Hymnal –
Natalie Sleeth's words and music, 1986)

This hymn, sung in mid-November, reminded me of the bulbs in our lives. Not only have we already ordered bulbs from our favorite catalogs months ago in order to ensure that we could get the selection we wanted to enhance our old reliables, but we have planted them by now. Thanksgiving usually marks unforgiving soil conditions. We have faith that those very strange looking clumps hold great promise. We plant them with a dose of bulb fertilizer and water them in. Then, we essentially walk away, busying ourselves with the final clean up chores in our gardens.

We trust that the challenging combination of cold and snow will enable a new spring of birth, greening, budding, and pow! – an explosion of color to banish the winter past. What many consider the sweetest season follows the most challenging.

Are our lives like this?

What bulbs have you planted years ago that
continue to "naturalize" and perform? In your garden?
In your life?

Do they need on-going nurture/fertilizer?

What bulbs have you planted this year to bring new
promise? In your garden? In your life?

What happens if we live in a climate that does not
experience the "cold and snow of winter?"
Garden climate? Personal climate?

Harbingers of ... Fall

We always think of harbingers in connection with spring, but the tell tale signs of fall are equal messengers: Dogwoods, Burning Bushes, and Evening Primroses begin to turn their scarlet hues. Swamp Maples ripen their reds and Birches add their yellow.

The delineation of the seasons is quite specific in New England. Not so our own seasons. Age is less a defining factor these days. Just as trees and plants have their variations, so do we humans. Once past the 35th reunion at college, we cease to be the peas in the pod we once were. Some gray early; others hide it or have genes that delay it. Some lose their physical agility, others their mental acuity. Some seem evergreen – looking almost the same as they did at graduation.

What personal harbingers have you noticed? For yourself? For others?

How do you greet these signs?

Have you maintained your core values, your sense of humor, and your caring response to others?

As John Donne knew centuries ago,
"Never send to know for whom the bell tolls ...
It tolls for thee."

Razzle-Dazzle

Late afternoons in autumn bring some of the brightest displays of light and color. Perhaps because we know that that warm tone will soon be replaced by the cold hues of winter, we notice the autumn rays spotlighting a yellow leaf as it twists and falls. On the pond's surface, I am particularly aware of the trail of glistening leaves mixed with the shimmer from the late afternoon breeze.

Much like "intimations of immortality" (learned long ago from William Wordsworth) and "Thanatopsis" (from William Cullen Bryant), these signs speak in a subliminal language. Those of us who are in the late autumn of our lives find ourselves choosing bright-colored garments (a complement to our hair and skin tones and our moods). It is a healthy response to the impending winter. Be gone, depression. Be gone, sadness. Rejoice in the here and now and the beauty that surrounds us.

If you or someone you know is a late autumn person, what are the philosophies and practices that demonstrate razzle-dazzle?

21

Remember George Bernard Shaw's desire:

"This is the true joy in life, the being used for a purpose recognized by yourself as a mighty one; the being thoroughly worn out before you are thrown on the scrap heap…" I quoted this at my retirement from federal service more than a decade ago, and physical challenges not withstanding, have attempted to practice this creed.

How does this fit with your philosophy?
How are you acting upon it?

In very practical ways, are you saving your "good silver" and china for special use only, or do you find yourself enjoying them more frequently just to relish their beauty (and build memories of their use for your children and grandchildren)?

Can we afford to be more lavish with our gifts (of all sorts) in this season?

Do we live life fully "every, every moment," as Emily comments in "Our Town?" My granddaughter Charlotte talks with glee about being with us for a "whole, whole week" – do we live with that excitement?

Scraggly Fall

Fall can be such a scraggly time in the garden. Shrubs are still sprouting ungainly branches that need trimming – especially if rain has been plentiful. Deadheading is a constant task for seeds to be saved. For other plants whose seeds the birds love, leaving the dark heads is an act of restraint that will be rewarded by the darting of Goldfinches as they visit the Coneflowers.

Biennials die off and need to be removed. Perennials that have finished blooming should be cut low for aesthetic reasons, but also to prevent rot.

Preparation to retire from one's job (if not one's vocation) entails similar approaches.

What to save?

What to trim?

What seeds to cast anew?

Remember to remove all of the invasive weeds and grass that can be seen more clearly when the garden is trimmed for fall. How does this apply in our life? Can we see the weeds more clearly and are we less inclined to tolerate their presence?

End-of-Season Chives

It takes disciplined perseverance to trim one's Chives, clear out all of the blossom stalks and other debris, cut off damaged ends, and then chop them into 3/8-inch pieces to freeze. Garlic Chives and their more mundane kin make wonderful additions to eggs, tabbouleh, cheese soufflés, garlic bread, and pseudo-Boursin cheese (see page 187 for the recipe).

I am always grateful throughout the winter that I have them readily available from my freezer, but inevitably I choose to do this task outdoors when it has begun to be nippy and they are in danger of frost. (Many were cut earlier in the summer to make my Boursin cheese, but then the heat was the issue!) It is tedious, but important work. It also neatens up the scraggly garden a bit.

What similar tasks do you perform in your garden?
If I worked indoors with favorite music, maybe
I could enjoy this task more – in spite of the
lingering scent that would result!

What tasks do you perform that remind you of the process and eventual delight in the product?

Making these preparations is a lot like financial planning, wills, setting up a trust, etc. It is not a lot of fun in the process, but the sense of accomplishment when done is noteworthy.

What conversations do we need to have with family members that resemble the Chive cleanup?

What other cleanup operations resemble this process? Have you cleaned out a parent's attic recently? Or your own? Do your grown kids still have boxes loitering in your storage spaces?

Autumn in the landscape and lifescape is a key time for such activities. A friend who works in the field of helping folks downsize their lifetime accumulations notes that two-to-three hours a day is the maximum. It is too overwhelming otherwise and the quality of the choices diminishes beyond that time frame. Having prepared our house to be painted almost in its entirety while we cruised off Tahiti and walked the beaches of Sanibel (yes – that is what kept me going!), I took three and a half months at the pace suggested by my wise friend to sort, toss, and store in the attic/basement, so that our painters had less to lift and put back in place. This included file cabinets full of 35 years' worth of research and writing about military families – my life's work. Additionally, it reminded me of closing up the homes of both sets of parents, so it had a huge emotional overload. But, we became gorgeous all at once at our house – a rare and wonderful experience!

The Leaves are Falling

Well, yes, it is sort of like "the sky is falling" of Chicken Little fame. Our vast green crown is quickly changing color, and then, after an incredible show of reds, crimsons, oranges, golds, yellows, and even burgundies, our crown is now a silhouette of branches. While there is beauty in these now bare branches, there is a visceral response to the reality of winter being on its way.

Those of us who live where this season of change is both glorious and prescient of a pseudo-death-to-come experience the extremities of the seasons more than those who pass through much more subtle climatic changes.

How does this affect our psyches?

How does it affect our rhythms of life? Leaf raking in the fall and the early spring clean up of the wind-blown residue are major activities in our neck of the woods.

On a lifescape vs. an annual cycle, how does autumn affect us? I find myself wanting to ensure that major maintenance projects are designed to last for "30 years." I want to take care of projects that I can do now, but may not be able to handle by myself in the years ahead.

Stop for a few minutes while you are raking and enjoy the glory of the day.

Parting is Such Sweet Sorrow

Gone are the delicious warm sunny afternoons at the pond. As winter looms, we are given episodes of sun filtering through the browns, oranges, golds, and burgundies of the tree-lined margins. The Japanese Maple shouts out, "Look at me!" All of the yellow Maple leaves on the tree above are gone, so the Japanese Maple has the solo position on the patio rock wall and exults in its spectacular color – a show stopper when sun beams focus their rays.

Nature seem to be saying, "I'm not going to sleep before I give a dazzling array for you earthlings to lock into your mind's eye." Or, to quote Robert Frost, "But I have promises to keep, and miles to go before I sleep." *(Stopping By Woods on a Snowy Evening)*

"Promises to keep… " I think I feel the need in the late autumn of my own life to dazzle, to say, "Remember me." It is a period of remarkable beauty. One harvests what one has sown, and then sows for the future. Psychologists call this our period of "generativity" – the time when we can ponder how best to pursue and support what we believe in.

My Monkshood is now in full bloom – gorgeous purple clusters on the top of four and a half foot stalks, mostly bare of leaves. It has spent all year growing for this extravaganza. The Winterberries are shedding their leaves for their spectacular display.

How do the Monkshood and Winterberry lessons apply to us?

Does the sorrow part of the equation intensify the sweetness? Bittersweet is aptly named.

Does a graying of your workforce or volunteer force cause you concern? Why?

Are your friends and relatives graying? What promises do you have to keep?

27

Harvest Moon

Shine on, shine on harvest moon....

Farmers, lovers, and motorists all find this glorious spectacle something that takes their breath away. Driving up a hill on I-95 in Connecticut, one is astounded at the crest to behold an unexpected huge orange moon. Drivers collectively slow to take in the view.

Whenever you are on water, the Harvest Moon is doubly magical. The reality plus the reflection is spectacular. It awakens a sense of the season departing, hopefully one that has been especially fruitful and productive, and reminds us of the long cold season ahead, when the moon seems smaller than usual and frigid in its whiteness.

What are the Harvest Moon occasions in your life?

Why do they seem larger than life?

What are the winter moments?

Can their crystalline clarity be used for good purposes?

Can winter be a season of internal productivity?

Winter Sunsets

Why is it that we especially treasure the blue and pink clouds as the sun sets in winter? We have certainly seen more brilliant hues in summer and fall. But, there is something about viewing the sunset through the leafless trees that adds glory to the experience. One of my favorite pieces of art is a silkscreen with just such a sunset through the silhouettes of trees. It has graced our dining room walls for decades.

Soon after my mother died in Tucson, Arizona, I sat on her balcony watching the sun go down. She had an enviable western vista of the mountains and the sun setting behind them. The copper mines' dust in the air enhanced the spectacle. We get so focused on our daily tasks that we often forget to witness nature's glory. That evening I did....

Even when we live in spectacularly beautiful settings, we can become accustomed to their presence and fail to stop and appreciate them. People in our community have often written in local newspapers about how the Mystic drawbridge gives them time to stop and notice our surroundings.

Mom used to fuss when the dinner hour at her congregate living facility conflicted with the sunset (or evening news on television). Choices have to be made...

How do we ensure that we make time for the experiences that cannot be repeated? How quickly the sunset fades....

Inspiration from Our Winter Garden

As we wander our gardens in winter, we see the forms and textures in ways that we rarely notice in the other seasons of our gardens (or lives).   When colorful blossoms (achievements and projects) are no longer the focus, we can appreciate the gifts that deciduous and evergreen plantings give to us.

We see the red stalks of the Dogwood bush. We see the curling bark of the River Birches. We see the pale beige leaves of the Beeches that hold on throughout the blasts of winter storms. We see the beauty of the ice-edged rocks on streamlets that we hardly knew were there in other seasons. We see dried grasses emerging from frozen shallow ponds. Leafless trees allow us to know the topography of the sites we drive by daily, never recognizing their undulations and glacial history. The now-visible rock walls remind us of endless labors past – boundaries built and fields cleared to be productive in this land of "stone flowers."

Lessons crowd into our consciousness. What design elements should we incorporate into our yards?

What design elements should we incorporate into our lives?

Should we plant for the winter of our lives? Should we have red Dogwood stalks to invigorate our perspectives?

Should we plant species that will draw others into our vistas? (e.g. Winterberries, Beautyberries, Sparkleberries, Inkberries, Alders, and Hollies to welcome birds and projects to entice others.) A friend recently has offered crochet lessons for a small group at church, with three outcomes in mind: the skill, the camaraderie, and baby blankets to share with newborns in marginal housing settings.

Invincible Summer

In the depth of winter, I finally learned that within me there lay an invincible summer. Albert Camus, Nobel Laureate

In the January 2011 issue of *Coastal Living* magazine, the masthead page featured the above quote, along with a photo of Penguins. In this year's particularly severe winter, this sentiment no doubt found resonance with many readers! Those who thrive in spite of winter's challenges do have an indomitable core that reassures them subconsciously that they will surmount the chilling effects of snow and ice. They will be able to survive the broken limbs and bent bushes. They have an internal warmth to conquer physical and psychological climates.

Do you have a sense of "invincible summer?"

Does that translate as optimism? Faith?

Does the experience of winter enable the discovery of one's "invincible summer?"

Is this indeed the gift of the season in one's garden and in one's life?

Gardening is Not for the Faint of Heart

The parallel truth is that <u>living</u> is not for the faint of heart! At the end of a day of readying just one of many garden beds for winter, plus planting bulbs in the anticipation of spring, I have very weary muscles (different ones from usual), plus amazement at how much really grew and blossomed this year, and the recognition that I have been blessed to participate so fully in nature's wonders. (Today is Thanksgiving Day.)

My favorite serrated clippers bit the dust, reducing me to scissors and, when necessary, heavy-duty shears. Tools are a really important part of our process.

What new tools do you need?

As you sort through your life (garden), how do you prune, clean out, divide, and yes, plant for the future?

Is it a wearying task?

Is it rewarding? Why?

Are there plants or experiences you will not reseed?

Even as spring promises to return, we sense that there will be opportunities in each day ahead to cultivate Wisdom, Beauty, and Diversity in our lives and gardens. Also, we should reseed Faith, Hope, and Charity.

Winter is Not for Wimps

Winter is both a season and a frame of mind. It takes courage to foresee the winter in our garden and in our life. Winterscaping takes planning, unlike other seasons when instant gratification may suffice. Warmer or younger seasons can be infused easily with transplants from friends and nurseries. Even autumn can be enhanced with buckets of forced Chrysanthemums, Coleus, and Asters.

But, winterscaping demands foresight: the planting of evergreens, berry-bearing Hollies, red-twigged deciduous bushes, and evergreen ground covers. Just as your winter garden needs pre-vision, your "vista vitae" (life view) needs design:

> *What are your economic evergreens and berries?*
>
> *What are your social-emotional evergreens and berries?*
>
> *What are your intellectual, aesthetic, and spiritual evergreens and berries?*

You recognized Abraham Maslow's Hierarchy in the questions, I am sure. If we want to be self-actualizing people, we must lay the groundwork every day. Malcolm Gladwell's book, *Outliers* (2008), accentuates the need to be involved and practicing our craft for at least 10,000 hours!

Yankee Magazine (March/April 2011) featured an article by Rebecca Rideout: "Goodbye to Winter." The subtitle illuminates our regional perspective: "An appreciation of 'the season of introspection' that only New Englanders may understand."

This book has been written in all seasons, but edited in the winter...

Pods in Winter

I have a wonderful book called *Pods: Wildflowers and Weeds in Their Final Beauty* by Jane Embertson (1979). It shows what the wildflowers look like in full bloom, and then their handsome fall-winter look. A real bonus is a picture of a dried arrangement featuring each.

Over the years, I have attended a number of parties that featured photos of the participants as babies, elementary school students, and even as brides. The theme of the "before and after" brings lots of "I can't believe it" remarks. Usually one can find the resemblance in the eyes and mouth, even if the hair is dramatically different.

The book accentuates the beauty of the pods... a perspective that delights us as we head into our own autumn and winter.

What key elements would be part of your pod?

When we are figuratively hung up to dry, what will be our value?

Some pods, like Teasel, are housed on very prickly stems, but are still collected for their beauty. Do you have a prickly stem? Beauty?

Some plants that bear a rather mundane flower are stars in their pod form. Are you such? Do you know people who fit this pattern?

The bottom line is that pods house seeds. What will be the seeds of your life to pass on?

What to Winter-Over?

Most of us have limited space to winter-over choice specimens inside (or at least in the garage windows). Those choices are always hard, based on space availability, difficulty in replacing the species, and their own hardiness factor. For those who have greenhouses, the space issue is less of a challenge.

My husband and I have made some unusual choices. He has various Ferns and Palms (started from seeds in some cases). We both love the chocolate Elephant Ears that send out many shoots in the summer, so extras can be nurtured through the winter. I have noticed that some of the variegated Geraniums are hard to find in our area, and they are fabulous paired in big pots with Begonias or Croton, so we nourish a few of those through the winter.

In our own lives, which are the special projects, programs, or interests that warrant TLC (tender loving care) so they can flourish again?

Are we attempting to cheat Mother Nature by coddling specimens that cannot make it on their own?

Can we cheat old age by coddling our specific projects and passions?

Someone said to me almost nine years ago, when we brought our newest Black Labrador home and into our lives, that I was too old to take on another puppy – that I should adopt an older dog from the pound. My nine-year old pulls me vigorously on daily walks in our neighborhood, weather permitting, and I am stronger and younger because of him. Obviously, we each have to evaluate our own hardiness factor.

P. S. I think I have <u>at</u> <u>least</u> one more puppy in me, but maybe not a Black Lab!

DESIGN...

Finding the Place Just Right

Horticultural nurseries and our personal travels expose us now to a panoply of plants and trees. When we are in the tropics, we envy the vibrant colors, exuberant vines, and fascinating Palm trees. Crowns of Thorns and structural Yuccas thrive. But, most do not transplant. Unless we grow some of the tropicals inside, they really do not fare well in our more northern zones.

Some years ago, *The News-Press** featured an article, "Water-saving beauties can enhance garden: Proper plantings are healthier, less subject to stress." Virginia A. Smith, the author, was clear about the bottom line:

No matter what the gardening problem, the remedies never seem to change: Good soil. Right plant, right place. And mulch like a maniac.

People are like that, too. We have social-emotional climates that could be as easily mapped as the USDA growing zones. (In fact, marketers profile us by our zip codes.) Can we, over time, adapt to the new zone? Yes, probably... and especially if there are micro-climates. But, if we are "designing with nature" à la Ian McHarg, we may be wise to plant ourselves where we can thrive.

> *When have you been uprooted and transplanted someplace new? What was your initial response?*
>
> *What is the human equivalent of mulch?*
>
> *Were you able to acclimate yourself? Were you able to thrive?*
>
> *If you thrived, what were the keys to your success?*
>
> *The old Shaker hymn, "Simple Gifts," reminds us "'tis a gift to come down where we ought to be."*

* *The News-Press* (Fort Myers, FL, Home & Garden section, April 5, 2008)

Size and Scope

Size is one of the major factors in gardening. It drives many of the choices we make, such as the size of plants, spacing, and selection of specimens.

Do you find delight in working with a very small space (such as a kitchen herb garden or a handkerchief garden), or do you relish the larger landscapes?

Is it a choice, or is it what comes with your "territory?"

Of course, if you do not have as much space as you would like, there are additional options: to rent space in a community garden, barter space in a neighbor's yard in return for maintenance tasks, or take on the responsibility for public spaces (such as church or post office gardens).

Is your garden ever "complete?"

How do your answers parallel the exigencies of the rest of your life? (e.g., work spaces, private spaces, and creative spaces)

Nature or Nurture?

That is the question... asked by parents, educators, and gardeners. How much difference do our efforts make with our progeny? If there were an easy answer, this dichotomy would have been resolved centuries ago. However, most researchers say about 50% - 50%. So, we have both hope and hubris enough to strive to make a difference.

If not for innovative botanists and educational psychologists, would we have been tempted to throw in the towel? Enough wrestling... it won't make any difference. But, the glass half-full folks say, let's keep nurturing the plants in our care. Translate plants to people of all ages.

Most gardeners believe we have an innate role in the design and care of our <u>plots.</u>

Are our soil "plots" our domain of nurturance, with a bow to nature?

Are our own personal life "plots" under our control?

When failures occur (and they will), how do we perceive them?

Will we try again?

Placement =
Art + Science

Gardeners face choices constantly about what to select for given spots in our gardens. Or, conversely, where we should put our newest acquisition. Yes, the County Extension Service and Master Gardener's training will help us use the science of soil, shade, and sun (the three S's), but the artist's eye also impacts the choice of site.

Selecting and placing new employees in the workplace, new volunteers, and new friends is a similar process. We can follow all of the human resources guidelines and studies of behavior patterns (*including mine), but we also are simply drawn to certain people (and plants).

Plants, like humans, prefer sun or shade. Selecting those that will thrive in your exposure is key. As you plan your landscape (and workplace), ensure that those who need sun (attention or acclamation) get the bright light they crave, while those who shun shimmer get the protection they need. Those who can produce with an alternation of praise and privacy will require your sensitive observation.

> *How much science and how much art/emotion factor in your selection and placement of plants?*
>
> *Ditto for employees? volunteers? friends?*

As these last three are people, not plants, we need to be mindful of our decision-making process. Transplanting or pruning people can be difficult.

Birds of a Feather: Lessons from the Sea uses the metaphors of the shore birds to explore the behavior patterns we encounter in ourselves, our family, our workplace, and wherever people gather together. The birds become a shorthand for the insights gained and the strategies for positive interface.

Exposure

Just as many plants do best in sunlight, so do we when exposed to experts in our field. New ideas and rules-of-thumb that we might not have been exposed to before shine upon us. Therefore, in addition to working in our own gardens, it is wise to read extensively, meet with others with shared passions, and seek training to advance our skills. One of the greatest opportunities is to visit others' gardens, open for special events. We learn a great deal that is local and specific to our micro-climate (and we help a good cause).

What do you read in terms of gardening?
Your profession?

What groups give you information on gardening?
Your profession?

What training or open house events can enhance your gardening knowledge? Your profession?

Learning to invest in our own expertise can be an exhilarating experience. Businesses that invest in training for their employees reap significant dividends – especially if the employees have had a role in selecting the training opportunities and if they are expected to share what they have learned with the rest of the staff when they return. Exposure to national experts enables us to assess our own quality of production as well as that of other attendees. It is one thing for your boss to praise his or her team; it is another to test that reality on a bigger stage. Exposure to excellence is a wise investment.

Garden Gates

There is something magical about gates in a garden. Is it because they close spaces in or people out? Is it because they provide stopping points where decisions are made to enter or leave? Do they frame vistas? Do they preclude vistas? We know well the lovely white-latticed gates with moon holes through which to peek. And we love the low gates that let us see what we are headed into with permission to enter.

In Charleston, South Carolina, gardens are often encased in hedges or fences with a gate, because the yards are long and narrow and abut the public sidewalks. Ditto lots of other historic settings in the South and the North... Newport, Rhode Island, comes to mind in our area. At our annual Mystic Outdoor Art Festival in August, paintings of gardens and gates abound. Clearly, they are a romantic motif. One of my all time favorite "gates" is in the Butchart Gardens in Victoria, British Columbia, where there is an incredible round space, very Oriental in origin, through which one peers at the inlet and pier beyond.

Our grandchildren love to remove the rudimentary gate to their granddad's vegetable garden – a world of high Tomatoes, Cucumbers, Peas, and Beans that climb his structural fencing... a veritable green fortress. That little gate is a dual use frame of hardware cloth – it keeps rabbits out of the garden, but doubles as a sifting device for the compost from our town's recycling center (the compost often has sticks and stones that should be removed).

A less magical attribute of gates is "boundaries." When I served as the director of a human services agency on a military base, I was introduced to the concept of "boundaries," something I really had not encountered other than tangentially in the rest of my life. I understood the rationale, but still believe that passageways, rather than boundaries, would be a more humane concept.

> *Do you have gates in your yard?*
> *What purpose(s) do they serve?*
>
> *Do you have gates in your personal life?*
> *What purpose(s) do they serve?*
>
> *Do you have gates and gatekeepers in your*
> *professional life?*

Garden Benches

Even on a snowy March day, there is something sculpturesque about a bench in the garden. It seems to say, "I am holding your place here, so when warmer weather comes, you may be my companion."

Benches serve as lures to quiet places in the summer, sites that almost enclose the one who curls up to read or daydream. A bench all to yourself permits new angles of vision with each position chosen. An invisible veil of privacy descends upon the recumbent figure on a bench.

In winter, with its arms and slats outlined in snow, a bench becomes a focal point as we scan the garden submerged in white. Its stiff bearing is a counterpoint to its summer allure. It serves as a solitary sentinel watching for warmer days to come.

Are your benches solely the sites of solitary musing, or do they sometimes enclose more than one?

Can they be perceived as safe havens for the occupants? Is there an unspoken rule that one's bench reveries should be undisturbed?

Have you placed benches to take advantage of niches or vistas?

Do you take the time to enjoy them? If not, perhaps some new rituals or traditions could be designed to incorporate them into your daily living… to admire what you have wrought.

Lights in the Garden

As I have traveled gardens hither and yon, I have always been intrigued by the lighting used. At Butchart Gardens in Victoria, there are many dear little low metal lights, some in an Oriental motif and others shaped like Lily-of-the-Valley blossoms. Some are solar and others work on electric timer strings. They provide a new way of enjoying the garden after dark.

Using idiosyncratic sculptures with lighting can be very effective. For years, our church bazaar attendees have asked if my faux topiary trees are for sale, and I have provided them with ordering information from Winterthur Gardens (I should get a commission!). My husband and I gave similar pseudo-variegated Holly topiaries to both of our moms. They left them on continuously in their congregate living facilities as beacons (for their arrival home after dinner and for finding their way in the middle of the night). Therefore, they lasted for half of forever. So, now I try to provide my own reproductions for the bazaar, hoping they will light others' lives "for half of forever."

One new project, courtesy of my husband's ingenuity, is a five-foot tall red wrought iron "tree" for our main entry (our back porch). It is an antique pot-holding tree – presumably for summer annuals in small pots. With Christmas tree lights wound strategically, it is a wonder to behold.

What items can you re-use?

How can creativity make the mundane magical?

Do you have co-conspirators? It helps if they are electrically gifted!

Add whimsy to your wish list.

47

Sculpture in the Garden

As storms threatened our region, I hurriedly tried to remove the top of the large Daphne/Dragonfly sculpture in our Mystic garden. It was our 40th wedding anniversary gift from our two children. The base pole would have its feet in increasingly wet soil and the top sculpture would make it top-heavy. The Dragonfly won – a slice across my brow ensued. But, the tetanus shot was within the decade, so only my vanity was wounded.

Sculptures can add metaphors to our botanical experiences, serving as exclamation points in both landscapes and lifescapes. A recent visit to the Coastal Maine Botanical Garden reminded me how sculpture can introduce and reinforce themes. The tall carved wolves and foxes were haunting reminders of the original (and continuing) inhabitants. The modern motion sculpture in the upper rock garden reminded visitors of the waves, both marine and wind, that impacted the gardens and our senses.

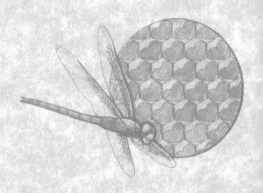

Do you incorporate any sculptures or works of art in your garden?

A mirror in a small garden can be very effective in increasing the size and contemplation of the space.

Do you incorporate any sculptures in your home decoration? workplace?

What is the impact of public works of art?

I am blessed to own the small trial bronze casting of a Great Blue Heron by the sculptor Elliott Offner for a Minneapolis setting – one of the National Endowment for the Arts-mandated public pieces of art when new construction occurred. Another of his Great Blue Herons lifts off from the pond at the Smith College Botanical Gardens and has become an emblem of delight for many students and alumnae. (The Great Blue Heron is the hero/heroine of my book, *Birds of a Feather: Lessons from the Sea* – an exploration of human behavior patterns via their shorebird prototypes.)

*Our son had kept the Daphne/Dragonfly sculpture at his house prior to its presentation, and he became so enamored of it that he ordered one for his own garden!

Green Fences

When our Mystic home was threatened many years ago by a connector road to I-95, I found myself "the unofficial leader of an unorganized group," according to the local newspaper! I also researched noise abatement and learned from a University of Nebraska study that I needed three tiers of protection: (1) at the edge of the road itself; (2) midway between the road and our house; and (3) beside the house itself.

The State of Connecticut agreed to copy on the connector side my pre-existing plantings along Route 1 (a green fence). So, they planted Yews, Junipers, a Sugar Maple, a Hickory, and Austrian Pines. My intermediary plantings were two rows of White Pines. And, next to the house were a variety of evergreen and deciduous bushes. Over the years, with cars stopping at both sides of our corner for the stoplight, we have experienced noise and chemical pollution. The Austrian Pines succumbed after about 20 years, but the Maple, Hickory, and evergreens have survived, albeit in an ungainly state. Because the State owns the small triangular piece created when the connector was built, and yet it provides no maintenance, we have become inadvertent "Adopt a Highway" caretakers.

When have national, state, or municipal decisions and policies impacted you?

Was there any win-win solution in the scenario?

What screens have you planted to protect your privacy?

What screens protect your project(s)?

Our neighbors have planted similar green fences on their roadside edges and folks in the community often comment on how lovely our succession of blooms is along Route 1 in the spring. Good fences can make good neighbors!

Creative Collaboration

"The rocks in your terraces came from the excavations for the shopping mall," explained our stonemason. We had heard from a previous owner of our pond property how thirty years ago he had stopped daily on his way home from work to load up his trunk with the best looking rocks for his extensive projects. Not only were we amazed by his feats, but we were also astonished by the stonemason's identification.

We put our faith plus crumbling banks and stairs in the stonemason's hands. As he and his team worked, they made suggestions about raising the height of the pond retaining wall, so that we could have a new stone patio level with our existing concrete open porch. Additional height at the water's edge gave us the perfect location for our pots plus insurance that grand-children and a Black Labrador would be "contained."

The rotting railroad ties that had framed our stairs beside the screened porch were replaced by large rocks, to naturalize with the existing wide blue-stone treads… a permanent solution and the new home of an array of Hostas.

How does it feel to have jobs done masterfully?

Such collaborations are more than a fee-for-service.
When have you formed relationships as a
result of a project?

How do you nurture the joint delight in a job not
only well done, but exquisitely done?

Have you been on the giving end?
What is "in it for you?"

Artists need consumers and praise. Sometimes, while we patrons are humbled by others' work, admiration is what keeps the creatives inspired.

Wind in the Willows

While we no longer have our Willow near the pond boat launch (it succumbed to old age and wind), we do have a number of plants at the lake that enjoy the afternoon prevailing wind. Begonias, Cosmos, Ostrich and Cinnamon Ferns, and our blood red Grasses all nod in response to the breeze. The heart-shaped leaves of the young Redbud that replaced the Willow flutter with delight.

All but the Redbud are at water's edge on the patio, so we enjoy them as we rest from our gardening labors. While their placement has been accidental as far as motion in the garden goes, I will be more intentional in the future.

What accidental choices have you made that brought unanticipated delight?

Will they become part of your purposeful repertoire in the future?

Some finely balanced sculptures also can respond to breezes for garden choreography.

More Than the Sum of Their Parts

Bulb companies urge us to plant clumps of the same species so that we get added "pow" for our money (and they sell more bulbs). It is true that the clumps pack more visual clout than a mix of variegated Rembrandts, though I cherish each and every one of their amazing patterns.

Artful gardeners also plant the same species or those with the same color in a rhythmic pattern in their beds. They are mindful when they select and place their new annuals or perennials.

We can do this in our lives as well. Instead of having a hodge-podge of activities and filling in randomly when time opens up, we can be mindful that clustered interests bring dividends in terms of impact.

What are your "big five" interests?

Do you consciously select companion commitments when time permits?

Would you accept just any botanical gifts offered or thrust upon you?

Are you strategic in your choice of activities?

Remember the concept of "creative balance" on page 5.

Random by Design

How do you sow? With precision or with calculated chaos? Are you measured, specific, and have a design in mind? Or do you have some areas where you can toss your seeds with abandon and relish the results?

At our pond house, there is a bank by the shed that was mounded up when someone carved out the boat launch area. When we first acquired the property, it was filled with invasive plants (Queen Anne's Lace and New England Asters) and grass. It also contained shards of pottery and glass. It looked like remnants of an old family dump site mixed with the ubiquitous rocks.

After several years of aching knees, I began to fill it with a few Cinnamon Ferns, Evening Primroses, Siberian Iris, Coneflowers, English Daisies, Spiderworts, Loosestrife, perennial Ageratum, Asters, Phlox, Columbine, Tiger Lilies, and Veronica. Each year in late spring, after removing the heavy clots of leaves and dumping tons of organic manure on it, I randomly toss the seeds lovingly collected during the previous seasons in Mystic and at the pond. I toss with great hopes that even a small percentage will find crevices where they can thrive.

How like teaching, parenting, and other creative endeavors...

Researchers have found that those who are truly successful in a variety of domains are not necessarily so remarkable except for two major traits: they are prolific and persistent in their dispersal of "seeds" — ideas, products, and initiatives of all sorts.

Years ago, when a much-contested (and detested) roadway was being built from I-95 into the heart of our village, my Girl Scout troop took the wildflower seeds they had carefully collected the previous fall from their family gardens and those of neighbors. They sprinkled them along the right-of-way randomly. A decade-plus later, one former Scout cut Black-eyed Susans there for her wedding bouquet. Sow and ye shall reap!

How do you sow?
With precision or with calculated chaos?

What seeds sown long ago have brought you
continued pleasure?

What initiatives begun long ago have brought
you continued pleasure?

Could you have forecast their longevity?
Their impact?

There are Times to Plan

When you know that long-term you want your gold-berried Hollies to be the focal spots in your house front landscape, you can plan to use some interim bushes to fill in while they grow. For example, our Forsythia, Variegated Euonymus bushes, and Inkberries can co-exist with the growing Hollies, if we keep them from overwhelming or crowding the Hollies. And, we must be ready to remove them when our Hollies have come into their own.

This concept translates to our own lives. We may know that there is a core competency that we are developing for the future. Meanwhile, we may also participate in some ancillary projects that can be growth producers, but can be removed/released when the core competency is ready to take the lead.

All of this takes planning, pruning, and awareness of the removal required when the focus needs to be on the key elements. Trimming and pruning are major sources of disagreement for my husband and me. He calls me "the butcher." Needless to say, our philosophies vary.

> *How does this planning/pruning concept apply to your life?*
>
> *What are your core competencies that you want as the key plantings in your lifescape?*
>
> *What are your disposable plantings that may give short-term benefits?*
>
> *Is your core competency worthy of your long-term investment in nurturance and protective planning?*
>
> *Will you reach a point when you reconsider your core competency and decide to plant anew?*

Gardens in Moonlight

Is there anything more magical than seeing our garden by the light of a full moon? Some gardeners design special areas of their yard as a "moon garden," featuring variegated Hostas with lots of white, Anemones, Hollyhocks, Astilbe, Marguerite Daisies, Clematis, Jasmine (*Moonbeam*), potted Orchids, and Bugbane (with feathery blooms in September). There is a ghost-like beauty to these plantings.

It takes a disciplined botanist to design such a setting. Hopefully, she hosts many gatherings on moonlit evenings to showcase her monochromatic montage. Low lighting can add light from the bottom-up to enhance the top-down view.

What other plants with white blossoms would you add in your climate?

What highly prized designs do you possess (botanical and otherwise)?

Do you share them?

What power does a restraint-specific design give you? (i.e., Discipline? Focus?)

A Bulbilicious Day

What a delight on this early day in March to see the little bulbs in the beds around the pond patio begin to shoot up. Because they are shallow, we cover them after planting in the fall with a hardware cloth screening laid flat to keep the Squirrels out. It is very effective prevention, but must be removed promptly to prevent entanglement once the green leaves emerge.

While relatively high in maintenance, these little bulbs reimburse my efforts with charming early color. They are warmed by the big stone retaining wall, the flagstones, and the high foundation and chimney wall. Sun is plentiful because the trees have not leafed out fully by the time they bloom. So these little hybrid bulbs thrive in their window of opportunity.

As with many human activities, timing and location are everything. The chorale with which I sing has found a similar niche this spring, giving a "chase away the winter blues" kind of concert in mid-March on a Sunday afternoon – in a church sanctuary where many families and seniors feel comfortable... a niche.

These niche plantings and activities do not usually happen by chance, more often by choice and strategic planning.

What are some examples of niche plantings in your garden?

What are some examples of niche activities in your personal life?

Professional life?

58

Butterfly Choreography

Today, our Mystic perennial Ageratum was alive with dancers. My husband and I felt as if our lunch on the patio was the setting of the "Waltz of the Butterflies."

Little white butterflies flitted amongst Swallowtails (both the yellow and black and the black and blue varieties). The Monarchs are yet to come. When they arrive, we become a carnival of orange, black, and lavender (the lavender being the Ageratum). The Goldfinches dart in and out of the oval clump, feeding on the Black-eyed Susan and Coneflower seeds that we have left for their pleasure. From our now shady patio, we observe these frolics in full sun.

Some would say that we are "lucky."

Some would say that we are "in the right place at the right time."

What is the difference?

Oh, by the way, we planted those Coneflowers, Black-eyed Susans, and Ageratum.

Incubation

There are some projects that fare better initially in small pot incubation vs. exposure to the full garden experience.

Because I have some tall, mature gardens, new starts need special care before they are introduced to them. For instance, a gift from a Women's Network realtor of Cosmos seeds prompted me to plant them in a pot in tandem with some Variegated Ginger (which was not thriving). They are now a Cosmos forest and could go in my main garden – or exhilarate in their current environment.

As managers (and/or parents), we have the same conundrum. Do we plant fragile new employees in the "big garden" or in a protected pot? Can we achieve a "Cosmos Forest" in a crowded, competitive workplace or can we nurture significant growth better in a protected spot?

Do satellite operations offer new talent the breadth/depth to expand? The concept of "skunk works" comes to mind – small groups formed to work discrete projects.

Nursery Purchases — Sinful Expenditures?

Every spring, my husband and I find that we have "nursery fever." His focus is primarily on vegetables, especially if his own starts from seeds have had mixed success. He always buys Lettuce and Pepper starts, plus some Tomatoes, Basil, and Parsley. But, he also looks for Cuphaea, whose bright red and purple blossoms brighten up pots on the pond wall.

I am drawn to Geraniums with variegated leaves, so they are cheerful even when not blooming. And, I look for replacements for last year's annuals and the perennials that have not survived the winter. I usually have some specific species in mind, but admit that I am susceptible to new ones. This year, a bright burgundy-red prolific bloomer, a Scabiosa Daisy, caught my eye for a pot at the pond.

Do you plan all of your purchases?

Are you open to chance encounters of the plant kind?

Is your plant philosophy consonant with your approach to the rest of your life?

How do you rationalize your expenditures for your garden? (Let me know — I need a few more good responses to my husband's inevitable question: "Where are you going to put it?")

Burgundy Accents

Over the years I have accumulated a number of burgundy-hued perennials to give my gardens and landscape depth and variety. The purple Smoke Bush provides a lovely counterpoint to the intensely pink Azalea in my front streetscape in Mystic. In arrangements, it also gives Redbud branches a rich back drop often accompanied by a white accent of some sort.

In my Mystic garden bed, there are a couple of burgundy-leafed Coral Bells, a dark-leafed Maltese Cross, and a Bugbane. The latter has a statuesque presence with feather-shaped white blossoms late in the season. It anchors an array of Black-eyed Susans, pink Coneflowers, and Cosmos. When dramatic bouquets are needed for end-of-summer garden parties, I trim the Bugbane and my equally dark Nine Bark bush, add some showy Hosta leaves, and all of the yellows I can find at the time (usually *Heliopsis,* Black-eyed Susans, and Spurge (*Eupatorium a. 'Purpurea'*).

Because we live in and near towns whose entrances are seen across waterways, I am conscious that the Copper Beeches and burgundy-leafed fruit trees provide artistic variety to their hillside vistas. Oriental Maples can provide similar richness.

What are the burgundy counterpoints in your professional life?

What are the Copper Beeches in your personal life?

If life is a bouquet, what are your showy blooms and what are your background accents?

A friend of mine, whose dad served as the arborist for the Naval Submarine Base New London (CT) many years ago, always loved walking around the base on her lunch hour. She shared her sense of connection with her dad's vision as she said, "My dad planted that Copper Beech..."

Happy Flowers

We all have favorites that seem to smile at us as they bloom. One of my favorite species is the Evening Primrose. Yes, I know it is invasive and I was forewarned by the donor. But the first painting I ever bought was of Evening Primroses on a simple canvas with white wood framing. The yellow "matting" was part of the palette knife painting, surrounding the yellows, chartreuse, red, and burnt umber (for stems and under leaf areas). I owned the painting before the flowers. I lost the painting in a lightning strike on our first Long Pond cabin, but the plants have been with me for more than 40 years!

Shared with friends, relatives, neighbors, and Navy wives, and transported to Virginia from Connecticut, they have brightened many a garden with their happy blossoms. In the fall, their leaves turn red and their seedpods are food for foraging birds and rodents… truly a plant for multiple seasons.

Do you know people like the Evening Primroses?

Is their optimism contagious?

Are they capable of adapting to almost any environment?

Is it worth allowing them areas in which to shine (even though you will have to weed them out and share when they spread too far)?

Or, is it easier to simply eradicate them from your garden/life? Does that actually work?

Extraordinaires

Our catalogs and nurseries are full of astounding colorations of both traditional and new species. Astonishing as some of the hues may be, we need to keep in mind the company they will keep.

If our intent is to put the audacious specimen in a space or pot of its own, then caution could perhaps be thrown to the wind. But, if we intend to insert a vibrant red or intense blue into existing plantings, we may need to be careful. The scintillating aqua-blue Delphinium always catches my eye in the nursery, but I recognize that it would have to be the star in an otherwise mono- or duo-chromatic design of whites and yellows.

My newest horticultural magazine has a squib about "a petite tree with exciting potential" – Redbud whose summer foliage "ranges in color from lemon-yellow to apricot or orange." It bears the usual fuchsia flowers in early spring on bare branches. This sherbet-colored tree would wreak havoc in my rose and pink-hued summer landscape. It would be a flashing neon sign of incompatibility. But, imagine its impact in environments that have lots of nooks and crannies to segment the vistas or a big space with a predominantly green backdrop.

My husband loves cultivating the "black" Elephant Ears, whose deep burgundy leaves punctuate their space, both by color and their tendency to dance in the slightest breeze. They do well in pots that can be placed so they capture the best light and do not compete with perennial plantings.

Have you been tempted to add extraordinaires to your design?

What precautions will you consider in your garden?

In your life?

In your workplace?

Exclamation Points

The Bellflowers, Blazing Star Liatris, and Yellow Baptisia are all looking like vertical accents in my Mystic garden. Other textures and shapes surround them, but their punctuation is clear.

Later, other exclamation points include my Bugbane 'Brunette,' Red-Hot Pokers, Cardinal Flowers/Lobelia and, some years, Foxtail Lilies. They add exuberance and height to my garden, looking almost like Fourth of July candle fireworks.

Do we have relationships with people who resemble exclamation points?

If so, what do they bring to our lives and organizations?

If not, why should we seek them out?

Do we ourselves resemble exclamation points? (I think I do!) If so, how is our exuberance received? Do we know when it is appropriate? Or not?

Do we choose our landscape design elements as mirrors of our own personalities or needs?

Supplemental Color

Insertions of colorful annuals can be made in two ways: planting them directly into the soil or planting them in their pots with their enriched soil. The latter solution works best in poor soil conditions and helps you water them specifically.

Insertions of perennials must lead, eventually, to permanent planting, unless you plan to over-winter them inside. They can be showy additions in patio pots while blooming the first season. By buying them on sale when they are performing, you ensure that your annual seasonal blooming cycle and color palette are synchronized.

Where else in life do we experience this seasonal supplement?

Our wardrobe?

Our menus? Entertaining?

Our reading?

Our business cycle?

While the insertion cycle may vary by season, the phenomenon is worthy of notice. We are typically filling a void of some sort, annually or perennially. Understand it for what it is – an intuitive reaction to a perceived "hole" in order to make a "whole."

Craving Pink

My mother's comment that I needed a pink tree in my Mystic yard reminded me of the glorious Redbuds I had known in northern Virginia and central Massachusetts. While I knew that she was picturing Crepe Myrtle, the ubiquitous pink in southern climes, I was surprised that local nurserymen said Redbuds were not hardy in Southeastern Connecticut. So, on my next consulting trip to Maryland, I bought one that has graced our yard for more than 20 years!

The Redbud displays her finery of pink tulle before there is any sign of leaves. Evanescent, the delicate blooms cry out for inclusion in a simple Oriental arrangement. When the leaves arrive, they are heart-shaped pendants that twist in the slightest breeze. The dance continues...yes, I want a Redbud in my life!

In mid-May, the variegated false Forget-me-nots have provided clumps of blue mist in my garden and the desire for a pink counterpoint becomes overwhelming. Invariably I buy pink/ magenta Cosmos to assuage my craving for pink, and the Royal Catchfly brings its fountain of pink mid-garden. My little perennial Sea Pink Thrift *(Armeria)* provides delicate pink pompoms at the front of the bed,

This pink component shows up in my trip wardrobes as well – pink or red to offset my cool colors or black & white. The mix and match scheme needs a warm component.

What other kinds of cravings do we experience?

While the pink craving is visual, are other senses prone to pursuing missing elements?

Have cravings been given a bum rap? Are there positive aspects of these longings?

Are they rational? Irrational?

Of Birds and Berries

This year our Winterberries have been absolutely spectacular. Non-descript deciduous bushes by our Mystic garage, they come into full glory in mid-December when all of their leaves fall to the ground. The branches, looking like Fourth-of-July sparklers, are laden with Chinese-red berries, made especially noteworthy by the white backdrop.

Usually, the berries go uneaten until hungry Robins appear in late January or early February. This allows me to cut branches for use with greens over the holidays. Not so this year, as a blizzard swept in a week before Christmas bringing 18 inches of snow. With the garage serving as a windbreak, flocks of Robins and Blackbirds joyfully feasted, reminding me graphically of the difference between aesthetics and survival. I have decided to forego bringing any berries inside this year, as this snow will continue to blanket the ground for many days to come, and the birds never seem to eat the berries taken back outside after their decorative stint is over.

Not that the Winterberries are the only berries in the yard. We have a smorgasbord to offer: Inkberries, Beautyberries, Swamp Alders, evergreen Hollies (even some with yellow berries), a few dried Crabapples, and the Yew berries. When times are tough, we need to ensure an ample supply of food. Beauty is a lovely bi-product, and there is nothing more beautiful than Winterberries filled with happy birds in a snowscape.

What bounty have you shared with others?

Do you include such bounty as part of your design?

Are you mindfully creating excess to share?

Have you been the recipient of others' bounty?

Hawthorn Heaven

Just before dusk this late January evening, the Hawthorn Tree is filled with Robins and one lone male Cardinal — too late in the day for me to enjoy the color of the berries played off against the birds. I remember the same Christmas-card scene almost four decades ago. Our neighbor across Route 1 had a mature Hawthorn that was filled with magic one wintry day. That precipitated my planting ours, hoping we could one day be host to a hungry multitude worthy of a Norman Rockwell painting.

This feeding comes with a bittersweet twist. Our recent heavy snowfalls have peeled back a major trunk with many branches – now carefully piled along both sides of our front walkway, awaiting removal. In the meantime, the berries on the cut branches are reaching a different clientele in our record-breaking zero temperatures.

When have experiences so moved you that you took action to provide something similar for the future?

What responsibility do we have to plant landscapes that feed our native wildlife?

What responsibility do we have to plant lifescapes/ways of living that will feed our community? What precisely does that mean?

P.S. The Robins came back the next morning and polished off all of the berries on the cut branches.

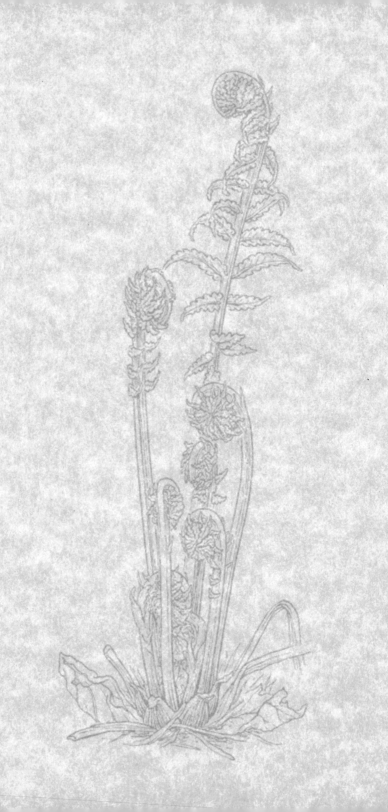

MAINTENANCE...

Planting and Maintenance

As it turns out, planting is the easier task. It is the on-going maintenance that requires greater attention over time: weeding, watering, and dead-heading. The last ensures continued blooms on annuals and perennials.

How similar this is to projects we initiate. It is fun to start something new, but continuing to monitor, trim, and support it can lack the initial excitement. And yet, perseverance is called for if successful outcomes are to be achieved.

What plants have we dug in and then failed to nurture?

What projects have we started with good intentions, but withered due to lack of attention?

What new relationships have suffered the same fate?

What lessons can we take away for the future?

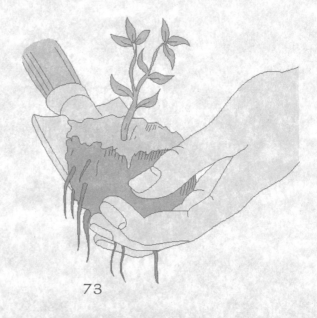

Priorities

When time is scarce for tending your garden, what tasks have the highest priorities? Most gardeners admit that watering and feeding are the top two, followed by weeding and trimming.

What constitutes watering in your garden of life? feeding?

How well do you fulfill these priorities? These are livelihood tasks.

Weeding and trimming are aesthetic tasks.

What are some of the weeds in your life? Do you get the roots so that they will not return, or do you simply remove the surface leaves?

Trimming can include the edging of your garden beds, as well as the deadheading that tidies up (and sometimes triggers re-blooming).

What do you trim and when?

Do you trim lightly, or do you cut back to fit a master plan or optimal size?

Do you find trimming a rewarding task or one you avoid?

What is your favorite time of day to be in your garden? Why? Does this come after you have finished other "duties" or not? What does this tell you about your priorities and/or your creative preferences?

Gloves

Gloves are to some gardeners what shoes were to Imelda Marcos! The variety and colors are functional fashion. Others wear gloves for medical reasons – if they have immune system challenges, gloves are a requisite first line of defense against infection. Still others attempt to avoid the dirt-stained fingernails that give us gardeners away.

Do you wear gloves to garden? Why or why not?

If you wear gloves, do you own a variety of pairs (or non-pairs!)? Why?

How do you store them?

What do gloves tell you about your approach to life?

*Hint: for pulling up the tiny starts of Poison Ivy under my Pine trees, I use disposable surgical gloves. They are thin enough for me to feel what I am pulling up, and I can pull them off inside out to throw away rather than risking getting any of the juice on my skin.

Spring Muscles

Do you suffer from "spring muscles?" You know, those muscles that have not been stretched by gardening since you put away the rakes in the fall? And now, eager to clear your beds in short order, you ask too much of yourself. Because the endorphins are flowing, we do not feel a thing until we come inside or until we wake up the next morning wondering why our body parts feel so sore.

Restraint is not one of my favorite concepts. Even though I know the phenomenon from decades of springs, my desire is unbridled each and every year. Clearly, the punishment is not sufficient to permanently implant wisdom in these matters. Uncovering just another small plot of plants, excitedly discovering what has survived and will thrive, brings more short-term delight than the not-very-distant pain can stifle.

Own up – do you get spring muscle pains?
Do you know better?

Is "restraint" in your vocabulary? If so, what was
the source of your learning?

In what domains other than gardening
are you equally prone to spring muscles?

Are they worth it?

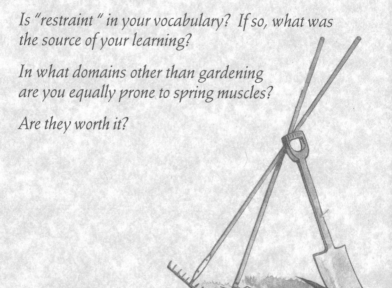

Soggy Soil

This is a dreary day in late February when the ice and snow have finally begun to recede from our lawn and gardens (and sidewalks!). What is left? Mud! Aside from the fact that it would be messy to walk on, it is in a terribly vulnerable condition. Signs should be posted: "Keep off the mud!" Our village has been undergoing "streetscape" construction, which has disrupted all of the curbs and adjacent grassy areas. They were seeded just before winter and now look like Paleolithic fossil footprint areas. What a mess they will be come spring.

The soggy soil is actually a mix of an under layer still frozen, plus an upper layer beginning to thaw. Because all sorts of roots, seeds, and rhizomes are in the varying levels of this striation, it is terribly important to be patient and careful in approaching the amalgam. Most recommend a hands- (and feet-) off restraint for now.

This condition reminds me of folks coming out of major challenges to their wellbeing. Those who have lost a loved one or have emerged from major surgery look a lot like these sensitive muddy domains.

How does this terrain relate to your garden?

How does this terrain relate to your physical experiences?

Your emotional terrain?

Those returning from combat fit this description perfectly. Post Traumatic Stress Disorder (PTSD) and Traumatic Brain Injury (TBI) indeed look and feel like emotional and intellectual mud.

KEEP OFF THE MUD!

Mulch

One of my landscape design friends has a license plate given to her by her kids: MULCH. Now there is a family that honors each other's passion!

Mulching is one of the BIG FOUR: watering, weeding, feeding, and mulching. Weed control and moisture retention are the two big benefits. Some gardeners also find mulch aesthetically pleasing – except the red variety that surrounds gas stations. In our seaside village, seaweed and pondweed are also viable no-cost options. Many towns operate recycling centers that turn last year's leaves and brush into free mulch. Likewise, woodchips. You supply the barrels, shovels, and labor...

Mulch can be both a protector and a medium for enrichment.

What is the human equivalent of mulch? Is it the interaction with others that occurs in our volunteer and professional settings? (e.g., our church hospitality hours, our business women's network, and our chamber of commerce before- and after-hours meetings?)

Are our media sources of information mulch?

Is mulch our personal blanket in which we envelope ourselves to warm/protect what we value and keep out the rest?

Making Supports Invisible

Some folks believe that one should not use any type of support in the garden. While I applaud these purists for their stance, I find that many of my plants will thrive if given a little support (and "guidance"). The Sages get leggy if not corralled. The Phlox and Shasta Daisies lean on each other after a heavy rain, causing a domino effect in the tall section of my garden. The Globe Thistle and Bugbane would take over every inch to which they could spread their branches, if allowed to do so.

Perhaps, if one's garden is extensive and each plant has lots of open space around it, it could "self-police" and not intrude upon its neighbors. But, in close confines, there definitely is creep. Most of us have fairly small gardens and live in relatively close confines with others.

How does this resemble your life?

What relationships call for support? In the family? In the workplace?

How can you make the supports you choose to supply invisible? In the garden?

In family relationships? In the workplace?

Are there those in your garden and your human life who are prone to creep? How can you control them?

Making the supports invisible is a courtesy, not a subterfuge. I have decided to spray paint some old white fencing a dark green – these 30-inch-tall metal sections provide the interlocking support system for my Phlox, Shasta Daisies, Siberian Iris, and Bee Balm. All of these tall plants tend to cascade as the season matures. Do you have similar challenges?

Nutrients

Nutrients for our plants come in natural and manufactured forms. Twice a year I spend the better part of a day at each house spreading a dried cow manure plus organic compost mix on my garden beds – in the spring, when the results are soon visible and then late summer/early fall, when the new little seedlings from my dead-headed perennials are first beginning to show. The key to the latter is that I must do it before the leaves begin to fall.

It is not fun and no one comes along and says, "Wow!" – at least not immediately. The fruits of my labor will take some time before being visible. Variations on this theme are sprinkling bulb toner and spreading lime on the lawn when our pH factor is wrong. All are labor intensive.

Nutrients for our own bodies and souls also come in natural and manufactured forms. One of the most "organic" and vital nutrients is pleasure. The endorphins generated by exercise, meditation, positive emotional ties to others, spiritual engagement, and creativity can help us be immune to disease and depression.

How does this act of providing garden nutrients parallel the need to fertilize the places where we work and volunteer?

How does this concept apply to raising children?

To making and keeping friendships?

To keeping marital and extended family relationships healthy?

Manure

Not the real stuff – the 40 lb. bag of organic "dry" (but usually not) manure. It takes a trowel to break it up, acrylic dipped gloves to crumble it apart, and sheer determination to give my gardens what they need to flourish…

The earth at the pond is glacial silt, with little or no nutrients, but endless mysterious root systems that web the near-surface everywhere. All I can really do is water and feed and hope that my rag-tag transplants can get good toe-holds in this mal-nutritional environment. The pond provides our water, so it is full of nutrients not found in city water.

The only meter that runs for the pond water is the electricity to power the pump. Many hours of hot dry days are spent watering – a pastime that allows me to weed with one hand and water with the other – and really enjoy my garden.

This fertilizing and watering also impacts my work – allowing me uninterrupted quiet time for contemplation and creativity. It forces a slowed pace… what is your equivalent?

Fertilizing and watering are activities necessary in our lives when we are between seasons, between events and activities. It is preparation for the gardens ahead (albeit unknown). What are the parallels in your professional life? Your personal life?

Have you ever lived or worked in the equivalent of glacial silt?

Bulb Food

We have ongoing opportunities to nurture the bulbs that we planted with such tender loving care. Not only can we feed the bulbs as we plant them, but again in the spring or summer when they reach six inches in height, and again after they have bloomed. So, life-cycle feeding is recommended for bulbs of all sorts, from tiny Scillas and Snowdrops (that never reach six inches!) to Caladia and Gladioli. Peonies and Anemones are also listed for feeding.

To what other botanical species do you give such care?

Do you follow the same regimen with projects that you initiate? Somehow it is easy to remember to nourish a new initiative, but I suspect that we may be less aware of the need to give support just prior to blooming.

The concept of feeding post-bloom has particular value for projects. What does that look like for your perennial undertakings? How is that an investment in the future?

Does this apply to human beings? Do we remember to nurture adolescents when they are gangly (physically and behaviorally, not to mention cognitively!)?

Do we nourish those who are past their prime? What expectations do we have for them? Can they still be fruitful?

Remember *The Longevity Project* mentioned on page 7.

Hose Guides

There is a fancy name for those wrought-iron embellishments designed to keep our hoses from slithering over precious Hostas and other strategically vulnerable plants – "cocks." But, "hose guides" it will be for now. Some are indeed wrought-iron Fleurs de Lis; but, others are simply found objects like iron pipes and aluminum gutter nails. Their function is to guide the hoses as we drag them to distant terrain to keep our gardens going. When others provide services in our yards, these are silent reminders.

We need the equivalents in many other arenas of our life. For example, when positioning my car to go into the garage, I point the nose at the handle of the adjacent garage so that my angle of entrance will help me avoid the woodwork and give me leeway to open my door.

What other kinds of "bumper guards" do we employ daily? Do smoke and carbon monoxide alarms provide similar services? Do key words keep certain websites inaccessible or, conversely, accessible? Passwords and PIN numbers of all sorts fall in this category. "Better safe than sorry" – not my favorite saying, has application here.

As gardeners, we are often reluctant to entrust our gardens' care to others. So, do we never go on vacation during gardening seasons, or do we seek others to cover?

Why are visible restraints effective in our garden?

In our lives? When that car maintenance symbol lights up on your dashboard, what do you do? When that pain, rough skin, lump, or weeping lesion appears, what do you do?

For those restraints that can be over-ridden, are we then given the responsibility when we make that choice? How has that played out in your life?

Untidiness

To dead-head or not? That is the question. For neatness of beds, for nudging new blooms, or to save seeds to sow anew, I have usually chosen to dead-head. However, last year the resident Goldfinches expressed such glee as our Globe Thistles, Black-eyed Susans, Cosmos, and Coneflowers were going to seed, that I decided to leave their feast untouched. My reward has been their trilling songs, their flashes of chartreuse and yellow, and their riding the heads with reckless abandon in the slightest breeze... a veritable rodeo.

My lesson – a little untidiness results in many seeds being sown by my feathered friends, plus the pleasure of their company. If I end up with too many errant starts, I will transplant them to appropriate locations.

When does tidiness in the landscape become a compulsion?

Does this disrupt potential delight?

When does control/tidiness in our personal lives become a compulsion?

Does this preclude some messy, unforeseen but memorable delights?

I know that my example will seem egregious to proper college administrators, but one of my favorite impromptu evenings at Smith College was the night a bunch of us "borrowed" the big metal dishwashing trays to go sledding on the hills around Paradise Pond. (Because all students in my era had squad/kitchen duty once a week, we were very familiar with those trays and they begged us to "repurpose" them!) Yes, we cleaned them up upon their return.

Thinning vs. Pruning

Pruning involves diminishing the height and width of plants and bushes. Thinning is a different procedure, often done to permit more sunlight to penetrate or to permit drivers to see oncoming cars through corner hedges without having to remove them altogether. Thinning requires a careful eye.

This is a strategy for our lives as well. It allows us to continue to be involved with causes and programs that we care about, but brings the discipline of being selective. When I retired from federal service, I decided that my ideal balance would include two national/international involvements, two local educational commitments, and no more than two roles in my church. Otherwise, there would be no time to write or garden!

While the commitments have varied over the last decade, the allotment has been constant, enabling me to say "Yes," "No," or "Maybe in a year when I finish…"

What thinning could you do?

What would be your ideal mix?

Would daylight, moonlight, and fresh air give you a new perspective?

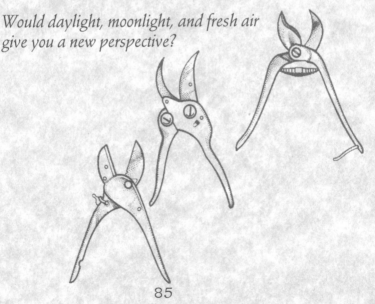

Patience and Perseverance = P²

My dad always relished the pun on the pronunciation of perseverance, with the accent on the second syllable: "Patience and perséverance made a Bishop of His Reverence."

These two are really opposites. Patience is a restraint, an almost passive state of waiting. Perseverance is an active pursuit or activity. The combination is more powerful than the sum of its parts.

Patience is a rare attribute these days, as instant gratification has become the major mode of behavior. But gardeners know that patience and perseverance can pay handsome dividends. As I observe the continued growth of Palms planted at our favorite beach cottage at Sanibel Island, Florida, I remember how catastrophic it seemed to lose two tall gracefully curved Palms a decade ago. The replacements, with Ixora at their base now blooming, are testimony to concerted watering by humans and heavens. Even bare twigs of Ixora, that I thought should have been removed when I saw them eight months ago, have leafed out and burst into clumps of red blossoms.

What in your garden resembles these plants? Your life?

Who provided the water?

Who had the faith to know that the plants or projects would become productive?

Have you experienced physical or emotional injuries that have responded to patience and perseverance?

Tiger Lilies

Such marvels of anticipatory reproduction are the towering Tigers! Before they burst into their vibrant orange blooms, they have already dispersed their seeds from their tall swaying stalks, thus ensuring their brilliant immortality. In wild settings, their presence is a stunning addition. In formal settings, their profusion must be precluded at their first sign, before their seeds develop.

Do you have similar plants in your garden?

What are similar experiences in our life? Habits? Relationships?

What casual uses of your time could threaten to consume your energies and preclude substantial accomplishments?

Weeding out invasive species takes discipline. How successful are you at this task?

Have you left a few wild places?

Resolutions

A January gardening article in our local weekly newspaper stressed the need "to grow a garden for health" in the new year, pointing out that gardening "teaches that much in life does not always give instantaneous rewards... rewards are often to be enjoyed in the future, like when you share a basket of just-picked beans with your neighbor." The author went on to quote the calories burned per hour in such garden activities as raking and bagging, weeding, digging, spading and tilling; and, the fact that women find gardening second only to weight training in boosting bone density.*

Most of us already recognize the body-building capacity of gardening, even if our bodies don't! We recognize the nutritional aspects of knowing where our food is coming from. But, the big next step is understanding the cumulative impact of time spent in planting and tending God's earth. I mean that both specifically and metaphorically.

As I delivered some materials from a local educational coalition to churches in the area last fall, I encountered a

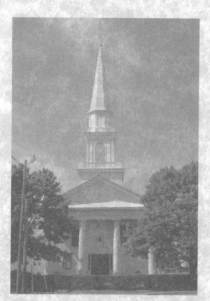

woman carefully cleaning up the extensive garden along a rock wall by her church parking lot. After dropping off my flyers, I stopped to commend her energy and commitment. She absolutely beamed.

88

I know that feeling, as I tend some of the gardens at my church in downtown Mystic. When the drawbridge goes up, the backed-up traffic stops right in front of my works-in-progress. With a sweatband around my head, a knee-replacement, and dirty gloves, I am not a raving beauty and hope that the local newspaper photographer is not among the crowd. But, you would be surprised how many people who are simply walking by or waiting for the bridge stop to say, "Good job!" I happen to think that obvious commitment to one's church, library, historical society, or service agency is good public relations – if we are recognizable to passers-by, even better.

Many garden clubs offer their services to community projects. Do you participate in similar beautification projects?

Often there are opportunities to do either long-term or short-term gardening projects. Which works best for you? Wise volunteer coordinators offer these options.

How can we help others learn the delights of such commitments?

I have tried to push the concept of "pocket gardens" at my church. The idea is that an individual or a family signs up to adopt one small area that they maintain at their convenience. All-church fall and spring clean-up days for major pruning, raking, edging, and mulching will still be necessary. But, the micro-gardening would make a big difference in our overall appearance.

* Diane Wright Hirsh, *"Knowledge to Grow On,"* Mystic River Press (Jan. 14, 2010)

Pachysandra:
Pride or Prejudice?

This remarkable groundcover has been hailed by those looking to decrease our mowed-lawn spaces, but has been decried by those who dislike its propensity to expand. "You will some day regret your plantings here," voiced our mailman in Arlington, Virginia, as I worked to knot and plant each stem given to me by my mother-in-law. We had bought a house a mile from the Pentagon, built in 1929, that desperately needed groundcover and landscaping. Pachysandra became a key ingredient in border areas with neighbors and in the shady back yard. These were not areas where shady perennials would thrive. When planted with peat moss and then watered well, it will manage in previously neglected areas. It resurrects barren spots and provides almost sculpturesque year-round groundcover.

> *Does it grow beyond its boundaries? Yes, eventually — and then you must cut it back.*
>
> *Can you reuse it elsewhere? Can you share it with others? (It is very expensive to buy at nurseries, so it makes a great contribution to community fairs and garden swaps.)*
>
> *Do you have talents that multiply their production in the same way?*
>
> *How can you cut them back, replant, or share them?*

There are other plants that fall in this category as well. Periwinkle outgrows its boundaries both above and below ground. It requires the same persistence by the gardener to prevent its becoming a pestilence. However, Bamboo really does fall in the pestilential domain. Its insidious march soon claims all adjacent space and precludes growth of anything in its path. Eradication is almost impossible, so beware of Greeks bearing gifts!

Raking Leaves

Raking leaves has become a sorting operation, because our town wants only leaves in one area of the dump. Another section is for brush, the catch-all name for everything from sticks, to branches, to stumps. Tree removal companies also bring loads of woodchips. The end products of each section are then available to citizens free of charge – compost, mulch, and woodchips. Citizens drop off their debris and pick up the reincarnated materials – a great service for ecologically-minded folks. The cost benefits are nice, too.

There are other domains that demand separation strategies. Certainly the recycling of bottles, cans, plastic, and paper requires careful sorting (and saves/earns the town significant amounts of money). Single stream recycling for these items is on the horizon.

Likewise, sorting through endless requests from charitable causes requires a disciplined approach. Each of us must select those we feel most passionate about and recycle the rest. Sorting through our options for entertainment and sources of news has become complicated. Nursery catalogs, just as all of the other catalogs we receive, give us endless choices.

How do you rake your leaves?

How do you make your choices?

Which things are not worth sorting?

Waste Not

Many of us grew up on "Waste not, want not." As children of parents who had experienced the Depression, we knew the many small ways in which they lived out this creed. Their mantra serves us well now both economically and ecologically.

My husband and I are enjoying our evening fires in the middle of winter, thanks to all of the twigs, branches, pine cones, and trunks of trees that met their demise in our yards. The wood was split and aged a year or so in our shed, that serves as the entry to our Mystic basement. Even in deep snows, therefore, the wood is accessible from inside.

By conserving raw materials at no cost, we benefit. What other fruits of our yards fit this category?

Or vice versa, grocery packaging that can be used for garden purposes? Do you use your fireplace ashes in your vegetable garden?

Are you able to capture rainfall and use it in your garden? We use pond water for our gardens vs. our well at the lake. The cost to pump the pond is much less ecologically than depleting the aquifer.

In early December each year, we invite our local garden club to trim evergreens that are overgrown on the parcel of state land adjacent to our property. This provides them with raw materials for their greens sale and helps us with the maintenance.

By using up and sharing, we have kept debris out of the recycle center and, in the case of the wood, have enjoyed its warmth. What else can be used up or shared?

Our Public Face

A man's home is his castle, but a woman's yard is her public face. There, for the whole world to see, one's landscape maintenance (or lack thereof) is a matter of public record. My husband and I live on a very public corner in Mystic, where one federal/state road intersects another. We abut Route 1 in front, so always feel under scrutiny when we trim the bushes, sweep the sidewalk and, yes, pick up endless cigarette butts (which are obviously too dirty for the owners' cars, but okay for our yard!). People stopped for the stoplight will often compliment our endeavors (or ask directions to a well-advertised lobster restaurant that is hard to find).

Frequently I hear from folks at church or in the neighborhood that they saw me pruning or mowing the bank. Some marvel, knowing that I have a new knee, but I think it is good exercise and am conscious of the appearance of a major corner in our town.

What are some of our other public faces?

Why do some care about their public face and others not?

Do the concepts of citizenship, neighborliness, and stewardship have meaning for us today? Increasingly, municipal departments and commissions are having to regulate some of those public faces. Zoning, derelict cars, and inappropriate clothing in schools and restaurants come to mind.

Who are the faceless generous souls who maintain the flower boxes downtown, the Post Office plantings, and the grounds of libraries and historic museums? They are key to our public face and we owe them a debt of gratitude.

Gardening as a Cumulative Experience

Gardening is a mix of cumulative and repetitive operations, plus new initiatives. The former constitute maintenance and the latter keep us engaged.

This rhythm of building and sustaining is true of other parts of our lives. While our choices of plantings do bring cumulative results, they are not "forever choices." If the accumulation becomes overgrown or unattractive, we can and should prune or remove. So, too, in life.

Sometimes it is easier to make this assessment about our landscape than it is to make similar decisions about our lifescape. Perhaps memories and emotions cloud our vision.

Do you find it difficult to clear out excess or unattractive plantings? Some find this an invigorating experience.

Are you loath to prune? Why or why not?

Does a new gardening year enable you to make a fresh start?

Does a new calendar year provide the same opportunity in your life?

Cumulative can be a positive or a negative. Do you truly cherish what you are doing? Your relationships? Or is it simply habit? Or inertia?

Moss – Almost Maintenance-Free

We are blessed with a hillside of Hair-cap Moss that leads up
to our meadow at the pond. Grandchildren love running barefoot
on it and playing a hilly game of croquet. It seems to thrive on our
poor glacial soil and soaks up every bit of rain and dew that comes
its way. In order to keep it looking good, I need to pull out
invasive grasses and weeds and pick up the endless debris from the
Oak tree. Otherwise, where a dead branch or an acorn sits too
long, the moss turns brown.

Native wildflowers, such as Trailing Arbutus and Lion's Foot,
erupt in the mossy spaces. Lady's Slippers emerge along the edges,
and errant Lilies of the Valley have to be mowed or dug up.
Mushrooms of incredible beauty dot the mossy hill, and Indian
Pipes appear on the leaf-rich margins.

Perhaps twice a year we mow the Moss, especially where it
transitions to the meadow, to prevent grass seeds from disbursing
and to have a uniform height. But, it certainly beats an urban lawn
for maintenance.

> *What do you have in your landscape that keeps you
> almost maintenance-free? Ground covers? Wildflowers?
> Ornamental grasses?*
>
> *What do you have in your life that is low maintenance?
> This category can include clothing that is washable vs. dry
> clean-only, low maintenance hairstyles and make-up (or
> lack thereof), and simple living practices of all sorts.*

We probably cannot reach a maintenance-free level, but can
strive for proximity to that goal. And then there is the wonderful,
musty, woodsy smell of moss after a rain. Get out your magnifier
and explore the wonder of this mini-world on your hands and
knees. It is a Lilliputian delight.

Less Is More

"Cleanliness is next to Godliness" – well, not exactly in a northern garden, because leaving a leaf or pine straw cover may protect tender perennials. Much as I am tempted to remove every last shred of debris as the frosts arrive, I know that natural litter can give beneficial warmth. Fortunately, the prevailing winds also ensure that what might have been almost-clean gardens soon have leaves, foot-long bean pods (from a neighbor's tree), and pine needles (from my trees) to cover the gardens before the blankets of snow arrive.

It turns out that a certain amount of detritus is beneficial. (Now, before your teenager says, "I told you so!," it is important that it not be harboring fungal growth or odors.) Some folks who are big into mulch know that it must be "clean mulch" – often hard to come by.

So, when you are tempted to be leaf-free, settle for less. It is a worthy accommodation that frees you up to do more important tasks.

When is some detritus beneficial in your garden?

Ditto in your life?

When is the drive for perfection a negative?

Debris from the Garden

Our town has a very enlightened debris-recycling program. We enjoy both getting rid of debris and picking up the resulting products, all for our annual fee, which also allows us to drop off construction materials, HAZMAT, and reuse items. This capacity has helped us clean out our garage, but has also replenished it with such items as garden chairs, tables, and an electronic organ!

Some horticulturists tout the composting of food items. However, if not handled correctly, these compost piles and bins can become havens for pests. Our neighborhood in Arlington, Virginia, was plagued by rats due to an ill-maintained compost heap by a USDA employee!

Where can you go in your region to dump items and retrieve others' "trash?"

What lessons here remind us to do our homework?

How does this apply to our workplace? (e.g., do we have a place to reuse/recycle office equipment and supplies?)

Do we recycle ideas?

Hallmark Cards has a charming center in Kansas City for children to enjoy the excesses of their production processes. School groups and individuals are welcome. Science museums have been known to let visitors fill a bag with manufacturers' odds and ends for a small fee.

Clean Up as You Go Along

How many of us heard this advice from our parents in regard to the kitchen and the workshop? This applies to our gardens and lives as well. Most of us do not have a sous chef to prep and clean up from our culinary adventures... or other adventures.

Perhaps one of gardening's greatest lessons is that when we trim bushes, we pick up the debris. When we have dead blossoms, we remove them to enhance future growth. When we have empty pots, we reuse or recycle them.

We take care of our tools. We keep them clean, dry, and sharp. When we have worked with diseased material, we clean our tools, gloves, and containers with bleach. This tidiness brings its own rewards. Our tools are ready and waiting when we need them.

Can you find what you need or want, and is it ready for use?

How does this apply to your work environment?

To your social environment?

To your spiritual/philosophical environment?

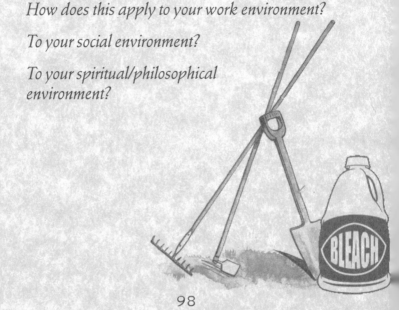

It is a Work in Progress

Or, it is never perfect all at one time! All of us who garden know this feeling. We work hard and at the end of the day, we presume others would not notice a difference. But, gardening is a cumulative venture, with incremental decisions and efforts making the significant difference. Layout, maintenance, watering, mulching, and feeding... continuously... are the key.

A friend confided today that she has all sorts of projects "out" to be completed, but she is frustrated by the lack of perceivable progress. I suspect it is a phenomenon to which many of us can relate. Busy people with a plethora of projects can feel overwhelmed when there is no visible sign of progress. It tests our stamina and commitment.

And yet, the weeds get fewer, the blossoms are more numerous, and the gardens are pleasing – if we can leave our perfectionist glasses behind.

We live here.

We grow here.

We learn here.

Whom are we pleasing? Ourselves and/or others?

Studies of those who have produced significant breakthroughs in all sorts of fields indicate that sheer perseverance is a huge factor in the ultimate result. Of course, it helps to persevere in a fruitful trajectory, but one can never be sure. Sometimes our paths are circular or seemingly random, and it is only in hindsight that we realize the cohesive patterns in our actions.

One Size Fits All

Not true! Finding the gardening tool that is right for you and having the courage to resist others' well-intentioned gifts or substitutions requires courage and persistence. This past fall, my husband decided that we needed new leaf rakes because our old rakes had been worn away on the right side (due to my use along the front walkway curb). He bought the huge, heavier, wider variety that I found difficult to use when I wanted to pick up a pile of leaves and put them in a trash barrel... too heavy and wide for my grasp and too wide to fit the barrel.

So, I have had to become a two-rake woman – a wide sweep for the initial raking and the old medium width for pick up. I had to preclude his getting rid of the tool that fits me.

> *How often does this tendency to mega-size impact our gardening choices?*
>
> *How can we notice and choose wisely?*
>
> *How does this paradigm play out in the rest of our life? (e.g., how much computer capacity do we really need? how big a package of food or dry goods can we use, much less store? how big a vehicle?)*

Cleaning Out the Potting Sheds

Yes, I have honest-to-goodness potting sheds in Mystic and at the pond. The Mystic version was part of an add-on of a two-car garage-cum-potting shed on the ground floor in the early 1970's. (Above, the master bedroom has a walk-in closet with two doors above the potting shed.) Both the potting shed and the closet are true luxuries.

At the pond, we originally used the former 1930's privy attached to the boat shed for our garden tools. When the whole shed had to be replaced, we used the same footprint and added a window in the "privy," plus shelves for my pots, jars of seeds, and bug repellants. Rakes and large tools hang from dowels on the side wall. My garden toolbox sits on top of my stool near the door.

Yes, it is wonderful to have a place dedicated to gardening at both houses. Sometimes, several seasons go by before I know that I <u>must</u> toss, rearrange, and clean my toolbox, gloves, markers, and seed containers.

How is this similar to the rest of our lives? Nothing disastrous will occur if we procrastinate, but how does this ordering affect our mental and emotional states?

Are we more efficient once cleaned up?

Do we honor the space and its function by giving it order?

Are there other spaces in our lives where such attention would reap benefits? Our office? Our family files? Our kitchen cupboards? Our pantry? Our linen and medicine cabinets/closets? Our community commitments?

The Good Enough Garden

Bruno Bettelheim wrote about "the good enough parent" to help us understand that perfection in this domain is both impossible and over-rated. The same precept is true as we nurture our gardens. We should exercise unconditional love of the plots we cultivate. There will be weeds that cannily outsmart us. There will be plants that fail to thrive as hoped. There will be species that, unbeknownst to us at planting time, become invasive. But, if we achieve an 80% success rate, we should be elated. Instead of being bothered by the 20% that disappoint us, we should delight in our bounty and beauty.

Many books have been written on the concept of choosing to push ahead and do the best we can do in a reasonable amount of time, and then moving on to the next opportunity. The desire for perfection can inhibit our productivity over the long haul because we may fine-tune something until it is overcome by events ("OBE"). We may also hesitate to risk, knowing that perfection will be difficult, if not impossible. In what instances is perfection requisite? Perhaps surgery, medicines, and nuclear power fall in this category!

How does this lesson apply to our professional life?

What personal applications do you see?

How often do we say to ourselves, "Well done, good and faithful servant?"

How often do we say this to others in one way or the other?

P.S. Martha Stewart herself, the doyenne of perfection, told us "not to worry about planting each bulb right-side up. They orient themselves naturally." (2011)

AQUISITION...

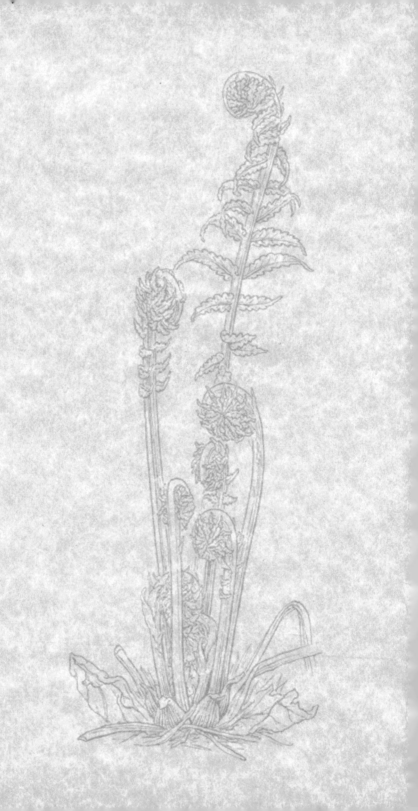

Spring Pink Fireworks

In my mostly bare spring garden, I have pink fireworks going on – Royal Catchfly is a remarkably showy fountain of blossoms. In spite of its less-than-engaging name, it has a formidable presence before much other than bulbs have assured me that abundance is on her way. She shines when the competition is absent or slow to produce.

Do you have similar plants in your garden?

Do you recognize human counterparts?

Can this become part of a personal strategy – to bloom when others are not?

Have you recognized perennial periods of low production that you could fill? (e.g., newspapers have periods when there is little community news being generated. Could you have PR articles ready to submit during these lulls? Could you offer to be a fill-in speaker if inclement weather precludes non-local presenters from arriving?)

Are there similar economic lulls of which you could take advantage? (e.g., providing warm-weather cruise-wear in cold climates when bathing suits are very hard to find, not to mention swim caps!)

Reaping
What We Sow

"Nothing ventured, nothing gained." How often have I used this refrain to explain why I have launched on yet another venture – be it botanical or professional? When I see a new plant that promises both late-winter-to-spring inside and then outside (Clerodendrum x *speciosum,'Java Red'*), I am immediately enraptured. "It will be gorgeous now in our dining room window and could be exciting on the pond patio, " I think. Large clusters of magenta blossoms, which match my Sarouk rug exactly, offset its coarse leaves. If it fails to transition the seasons, I have at least had the pleasure of its company for now (at half price!).

If I do not try new approaches in other realms of my life, what have I lost?

How does this philosophy apply to our garden?

To our creative life?

To our professional life?

What have we sown in our relational lives?
And what do we reap?

Lunaria Lust

Thou shalt not covet thy neighbors'... Lunaria. But, I do!
They have the healthiest, most gorgeous stand of the purple
Money Plant, named in Latin for the moon because its seedpods
are covered with parchment circles. When dry, the pods reflect
the moonlight like little moons.

But, it is their purple blossoms that are "fun-nomenal." The
plants are gangly and clearly not meant for polite company, but
the blossoms form handsome clusters. Lunaria like roadside areas
where leaf mulch and moisture accumulate. My neighbors
provide a similar environment with their mulch pile of grass and
leaves along their driveway.

I transplanted some that were inappropriate in our church
landscape, but the plants did not thrive – the usual case, I know.
However, they continue to propagate at the church where I do
not want them – perverse! Ornery! So, I've cut up endless dried
seedpods and scattered them at the pond. If they thrive there,
they would be in a wild area. I hope they find a home – my
home!

Have you struggled with wild plants and wild ideas?

Have you struggled with envy?

What strategies worked?

P.S. Guess what I found today!
One small, but vital Lunaria in our far
back yard in Mystic. Now, for patience...

P. P. S. Delicious metaphorical
irony: another name for the
plant is "Honesty."

107

End of Summer "Pow"

Two end-of-summer perennials cried out to me at the nursery, "Take me home! I could add super color to your flagging beds." A huge Gay Feather *(Liatris)* and a short, sturdy Sunflower (some of whose blossoms were already going to seed) found their way into my cart. I kept the seeds of the latter and sprinkled them generously in my cutting flower oval in Mystic and at the pond.

Years ago, in order to beef up my garden before our daughter's wedding on Columbus Day weekend, I bought low, densely purple Asters and Montauk Daisies. We still have both 16 years later. The Montauks have been transplanted twice, as they needed more space, even with early season trimming. The Asters occupy their original site and are glorious reminders of a happy day.

Do you have "event plantings?"

I still have Stargazer Lilies from friends at cancer surgery time. They remind me of the event, but also the friends who knew I would appreciate them for more than a decade.

A pink Azalea given to me for my 60th birthday by my staff at work (who knew how I loved gardening and had often visited the pond), struggled at first in our tough soil there, but with lots of TLC is flourishing – and so is my life, more than a decade later.

"Say it with flowers" is quite the marketing tool, but also can be especially meaningful as we face the fall of our lives.

108

Beautyberry

What a pretentious name, but what an accurate description. Purple Beautyberry is a bush, which can become a ten-foot tree in older specimens. It has small chartreuse leaves, but its crowning glory is a row of tiny, intensely purple berries that line the top of the bract in the fall and become noticeable once the leaves fall. "Profusion" is the self-pollinating cultivar.

The berries really are too fragile to use in a bouquet, prone to rolling off everywhere. So, their primary uses are human delight and food for birds in the neighborhood. After seeing them on various autumn house tours, I knew that I had to have one. It sits right where I pass it each morning, after retrieving the morning newspaper with my dog from the front lawn. Seeing it brings a smile and I know that our resident Cardinals and Catbirds have it spotted. Now, if we lived in the South, the snakes would also know that when the berries are ripe, the birds can get drunk and careless! Pyracantha berries play the same role, and the neighborhood cats replace the snakes as the raucous bird consumption ritual begins.

What human events and celebrations are just beautiful on their own terms and too fragile to remove to an arranged setting?

Does the Beautyberry remind us of the "Ugly Duckling" story? How many other plants resemble this theme?

How many of us or our projects resemble this theme?

Who are some of the Swans you know?

Annual vs.
Hardy Tulip Bulbs

Only recently have "hardy Tulips" become readily available. Unlike their large, showy annual relatives, they are plainer and smaller. Some of the very small species have beautiful little blossoms, but they can be overwhelmed by neighboring plantings if the gardener is not careful.

Some of the medium-sized hardy bulbs produce only solid colors, so the gardener must choose between glamorous annuals and less showy quasi-perennials. That choice is often paralleled in our own lives.

What do you consider your perennial achievements?

Have you made a trade-off between predictable moderate blossoms and less reliable, but exciting potentialities?

Do you have a mix of these in your life?

Could this phenomenon describe acquaintances vs. friendships?

I must confess to my discomfort when I see public gardens planted with a huge display of the same species of tulips – truly impressive en masse – but then weeks later, the gardeners remove every single bulb, knowing that their repeat performance would be half at most the following year, and then maybe half of that the year thereafter. It seems like such an effort to produce evanescent beauty, but there are others who relish the short-lived glory.

Garden Bags and Pots

When new plants come in plastic pots and mulch, lime, and fertilizer bring plastic bags to your household, what can you do with them? If the pots carry the recycle symbol, either re-use them for your own purposes or put them in the recycle bin. The bags are harder – they can have second lives in the pet poop pail; they can be laid on the garden and covered with mulch to curtail weeds; or they can be used to contain raked leaves and make many emptying trips to your town leaf recycling center.

Ideally, you would buy your plants and products in wrappers that are biodegradable – recycled paper pots and paper bags.

When you purchase products of all sorts, think about the implications of the packaging. If you return your plastic garden trays to your nursery and comment that a paper tray would be preferred, they will take notice.

Ditto pots and bags.

Gardeners, of all people, should appreciate when their bulbs come in recycled paper boxes and are packed with shredded cardboard or catalog strips vs. foam peanuts.

In what other ways can you be an activist? Are there habits that you can transfer from your gardening world to other shopping? Can you use gardening carts, trays, and baskets/trugs to transport items for other purposes?

One Woman's Excess = Another's Treasure

Avocado starts, rooted Aucuba, excess perennial Ageratum, and a Scotch Broom that was disrupting a pathway at the pond all found new homes this week. I cannot bear to throw them away, knowing that someone will want them. Likewise, I was the recipient earlier this year of a friend's excess Bellflowers and Lady's Mantle – treasures indeed for my pond gardens.

Recently a friend asked me to come look at her attic gift box for possible ingredients for the gift baskets we make up for our annual church bazaar. A survey that we conducted several years ago about what our congregation wanted most demonstrated that gift/hostess baskets already wrapped and ready to go would be a popular item. My friend's treasures will be carefully combined with other new items to make intriguing assortments.

She and I relish our ability to repurpose pretty and useful things to bring pleasure to someone else – both the purchaser and the recipient. Being creative and frugal at the same time allows us to raise funds for local charities, hence increasing our positive impact.

What plants do you have that enable sharing?

What projects do you have that enable sharing?

Are you able to rejoice in the reuse (vs. guilt about passing them on)?

Do these efforts also help you to reduce your consumption, acquiring less at the outset? Or at least reduce your outlay?

Vessels

As evening sets, my two large blue glass bowls on the radiator cover behind the piano bench look out on a snow-covered view of Yew, Magnolia, and Pine. And pine they do for warmer weather, to be filled with Redbud, Crabapple, and Smoke Tree branches. I think the tall blue globe also longs for stems of Calla Lilies and Gladioli.

The second bowl, a "could-be" wine cooler in gradations of blue and clear glass, has nurtured many Aucuba rootings. It is especially well suited for this task, as the rootings thrive when sunlight can reach them.

Do our vessels nudge us towards finding treasures for them to hold?

How can empty vessels long?

How can we long?

Do we know what we are meant for?

And what we are missing?

Winterberries vs. Sparkleberries

Winterberries and Sparkleberries are deciduous Hollies. The former requires a male and a female plant in order to bear berries, while the Sparkleberries are bi-sexual. They are self-pollinating (with the help of friendly bees, etc.)

The Winterberries tend to have bigger berries that are a Chinese red. The Sparkleberries tend to be a bit smaller and a little more orange in color. The big advantage of the Sparkleberry is that you need only one bush which, in all honesty, is scraggly looking until it loses its leaves and shows its berries. Ditto the Winterberry female.

How many of us feel a little scraggly before our prime? If you have been to college reunions, the recent classes tend toward the scraggly and the later classes seem to have gotten their act together (fashion and otherwise).

What are the benefits/detractors of a solo operation?

What are the pros/cons of a dyad?

Could you have both in your landscape? Lifescape?

Self-Sowers

Plants that self-sow can be a blessing or a bane, depending upon our perspective and our plans for given spaces. Most gardeners know that they can deter an overabundance of self-sewn starts by deadheading methodically. I see them as gifts – those Feverfews, Black-eyed Susans, Columbine, and Campion – in fact, I often aid in their dispersal. Especially at the pond, I am grateful for almost everything that appears, except the ubiquitous Hawkweed that makes itself at home in lawns as well as garden beds.

The self-sowers add a relaxed, casual mix to my garden beds. More informal than formal gardeners might prefer, they are the folks who stop to chat when they see you outside. They are the casual encounters at the supermarket who are pleased to see you and add a quick compliment to your day. Just as the self-sewn plants, these folks are generous, seeing their plenitude as reason enough to share.

Interestingly enough, not all species that typically are self-sowers will thrive in your garden – the conditions are not favorable to all. I love Purpletop Vervain (*Verbena bonariensis*), but even with several gifts of large clumps from friends whose gardens were overrun, I have none showing this year.

Perhaps certain workplaces are more conducive to self-sowers than others.

Perhaps personal as well as botanical boundaries are necessary to contain or preclude certain species.

Far from miserly with their gifts, self-sowers may overwhelm us. Do you know any such?

If you are a self-sower, what lessons have you learned?

115

Seeds and Rootings

My husband methodically collects the seeds from our various showy Hostas to propagate plants to share. This summer our two children and their families gleefully took home their "Sum and Substance" pots after seeing the huge adult plants in Mystic and at the pond.

Likewise, we collect the seeds from our Salad Burnet plants each year, because they are plentiful in our herb garden and hard to find in nurseries, either as seeds or as starts. Salad Burnet provides an unusual cucumber-like flavor to salads and cheese spreads. It also shares with Lady's Mantle the phenomenon of water droplets glistening on the leaves. For our most recent church bazaar, I·made up small packets of seeds to sell for a dollar each and they flew off the table.

I trim our Aucuba bushes to keep them shapely and to provide greens for my winter arrangements. Aucuba is an evergreen with yellow speckles on fleshy leaves. It behaves a lot like Rhododendron, with leaves curling up when the temperatures hit 20° and below. Our area is marginal for their survival, but with careful siting, they continue to thrive. They are "heritage plants" from my in-laws in Arlington, Virginia.

Other in-law heritage plants include variegated Hostas and Pachysandra. We have populated our terraces at the pond with the hardy Hostas and have given a bunch to our son for his challenging terraces. The Pachysandra, which some gardeners come to hate because it can take over, has filled in many curving beds in Mystic and at the pond. It is low maintenance and gives a gracious maturity to our yards.

What are the garden projects that you similarly coddle?

Are there other products that you nurture for which you must insure the raw materials?

Are you involved in mentoring?

How can we plant the seeds and share the rootings with others so that heritage and legacy thrive (not just survive)?

Are there giant steps that we can take to protect historic and environmentally sensitive sites for perpetuity?

This activity reminds us that we must sow in order to reap. And, then, the follow-on precept is that we must reap in order to sow.

Locaflor

Just as many are learning the value of consuming foods grown locally, we gardeners may want to focus our purchases on regional stock. That way, we can select the healthiest specimens and ensure safe transportation to our planting sites. Additionally, local growers may be better attuned to the micro-environments in which we garden, so their advice on sustainability could be more pertinent than the classic USDA zone map (U. S. Department of Agriculture map used by most inter-state plant shippers).

Catalogs abound and are very tempting resources. Perhaps seeds and bulbs could be safely shipped. However, my experience with bare root and potted plants has brought mixed results. Especially unreliable for me are plants encased in fancy bags and boxes sold at big box stores. Although the grower did make good on the guaranteed replacement of plants that failed to thrive, I am now inclined to invest in what I can see and determine its quality of previous care.

Often, local garden clubs, historical gardens, and library fairs feature members' garden excesses. The price is usually right and some percentage of the purchase total may be tax deductible.

The parallel to the "locavore" movement is clear. In what other categories could local be more reliable than purchases from afar?

How about hiring new employees? Are local references more reliable than those farther afield whose caliber may be hard to determine?

Friendship Gardens

When I work in my pond and Mystic gardens, I am surrounded by friends – or at least the plants they have given to me. When we first moved to Mystic four decades ago, neighbors knew that I was starting from scratch in what clearly had become a dumping area for previous occupants. They commented that I would need a "friendship garden" and promptly provided me with my first gifts.

As the years went by, I shared my excesses with Navy wives new to the area and sister gardeners. My mother-in-law brought me Hostas and Pachysandra from her Arlington, Virginia, yard and wild Dogwoods from her former neighbor. A sister teacher/ counselor shared her Scotch Broom starts and Siberian Iris, originally from her family's Michigan home. One especially good friend supplied me with perennial Ageratum from her aunt's New York garden and, as written elsewhere, her Sweet Woodruff, tall yellow daisies, and lots of little decorative grasses for a pond bank. However, her best early spring gift was something she called "Baby Blue Eyes," actually *Veronica 'Bergen's Blue.'* It has naturalized in several difficult spots at the pond and blooms its heart out in tandem with our little hybrid bulbs. It has even thrived where the Creeping Phlox has waned.

What have you received and given botanically?

Do you save clumps to share with annual not-for-profit fairs as fund-raisers?

Do you have the equivalent experience in other domains? (e.g., tag sales, silent auctions, church bazaars, etc.)

Have some of your plants' donors died? How does having their stock heal, bring good memories?

Have some of your relationships migrated or declined? How does your botanical awareness help with that phenomenon?

119

Fashion and Flowers

Flowers and gardens are as subject to fashion trends as many other elements of our culture, but not quite as fast on the turnaround as women's clothing. There are a number of factors driving this phenomenon, including the global availability of cut flowers, bulbs, seeds, and rooted species. If you live near major flower markets, you can have almost anything you want in any season from anywhere in the world.

At the same time, there is a return to vintage species. Historic museum gardens want to be true to their botanic period and many locavores are interested in heritage vegetables (tomato species come to mind). Availability does not guarantee *thrivability* (I know – it is a new word, but an old concept).

Think about your favorite garden magazines. Are they cutting edge or traditional in flavor?

Examine your garden catalogs for indicators of their point of view. Their graphic design is usually a giveaway.

Would you enjoy working with exotic flowers for arrangements vs. planting them in your garden (i.e., short term vs. long term choices)?

How do fashion trends impact your botanical arrangement and garden design? Your professional and personal choices?

TOOLS...

Tool Bag vs Tool Box

The decorative tool bags with multiple pockets for tools and gloves come in enchanting fabrics or serious eco-colors. They always look like fun gifts.

But my heart belongs to the heavy wooden tool boxes that my husband helped our Girl Scout troop (all 22 of them!) make for their mom or dad one Christmas. Mine has a slot on the handle to drape my gloves through to dry. I can see all of my heavy tools readily and can tie on a plastic bag for non-garden debris when I work on the church plantings. Once or twice a year, I have to remove all of the tools and dump the accumulated dirt. It is a personal preference thing.

What gardening preferences do you have?

Are there some items for which you need to know others' habits before giving? (e.g. for gardening, cooking, etc.?)

Do your senses play a role in your preferences? (e.g., scent, taste, perception of colors, etc.?)

Do cultural and educational backgrounds impact your choices?

Tools of My Dreams

I once told a friend that the tool of my dreams would be a combination of serrated clippers on one end and a weeder on the other. That way, when I've finally found a spot to stand in my garden and bend to clip or weed, I wouldn't need a tool belt to avoid leaving the hard-won position. (With a new knee, this is more important than ever! My balance and agility for hopping over the garden fencing are not what they used to be... for a while anyway.) Because no one is manufacturing my dream tool, I am reduced to a very bad habit of using the clippers closed as a weeder – which, of course, dulls them and forces me to look for a new pair. My friend laughed at my vision!

One tool that I do think is wonderful is the "multi-purpose garden knife," which combines a slightly curved stainless steel blade with a ruler marked on it. The blade has one serrated edge and one straight sharp edge with a slot for cutting twine. The serrated edge is particularly helpful with roots in a bulb hole. At the tip, there is a V-slot for weeding.

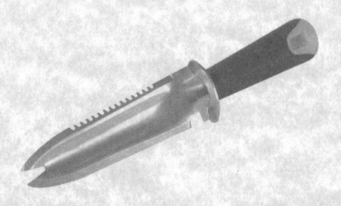

Why doesn't some enterprising gardener come up with the equivalent of a Swiss Army gardening tool? Yes, it would be more bulky than its prototype, but it would save a lot of steps back to the toolbox. The implements should be extractible by someone wearing gloves, don't you think?

What components would your Swiss Army garden tool include?

Are there other areas of your life that could benefit from a multi-task tool? For example, a whisk on one end and a rubber spatula on the other?

Are there people you know who resemble the single task and multi-capable tools? Both in the way they think and behave?

If you have limited space and funding in your workplace, whom will you hire – the single task or multi-task individual?

Trick question: if you have plenty of space and funding, whom will you hire? And why?

Christmas Stocking Stuffers

My husband says, "We are of an age when consumables are the best gifts." Well, I consider gardening gloves and some tools "consumables." I go through gardening gloves like there's no tomorrow. So, two pairs of latex-dipped gloves and two cotton pairs would be a start. Remember, I have two locations at which I garden.

My serrated grass shears not only trim the grass along the sidewalks and garden beds, but also chop back Phlox, Iris, and Ageratum in the fall. It is impossible to really sharpen them, so a new pair every other year would be greatly appreciated. Garden twine, identification markers for new species or to remind me of the exact location of some of my favorites, and green metal support rings would also be welcome.

A spring bulb catalog with a gift certificate would allow pleasurable choices in the middle of winter. Other IOU's for plants come spring or specialty vegetable seeds would also be nice thoughts. A good photo album that allows notations beside each photo enables good record keeping and on-going delight. A cruise to the "Private Gardens of the Caribbean" would be a super-nice gesture! You see, gardeners really are very easy to shop for!

What would you add to this list?

Are there special tools that you would want to pick out yourself (so an IOU would be preferable)?

Are there books that you have wished for? Magazine subscriptions?

How do these categories apply to other interests (for you or others)?

Shortcuts

When you hear the word "shortcut," what do you think? Efficient? Diminished value? Innovative? Breaking traditions? More time to do something you enjoy?

An electric hedge trimmer can make fast work of perennial plants at the end of the season. Our cutting bed of Ageratum, Coneflowers, and Black-eyed Susans needs to be chopped back and cleaned out before we can plant our new bulbs. Another area of Phlox, Shasta Daisies, Bee Balm, and Siberian Iris is a good candidate for the trimmer.

Other areas require the traditional, back-breaking, hands-on approach. When trimming bushes, we are selective in our use of the trimmer. My personal preference is not the sculptured Italian garden look. For Mountain Laurel and the variegated Euonymus bushes, I prefer the careful hand pruning techniques. However, our ground cover Euonymus is evened up with a trimmer in no time – three times a year!

For the spring garden, my husband has built a frame with two chicken wire "shelves" supported by crossbeams. Once the tomato plants have grown beyond their individual cages, they reach up into the two shelves for support. It is easy to spot and pick the ripe fruit.

Choices!
When does efficiency not impact quality?

In your kitchen?
In your sewing or craft room?
In the garage or workshop?
In your workplace?

Awesome Auger

Having the right tools for the job makes all of the difference in the world. After having owned a 2 3/4" awl for making holes for big bulbs, like Tulips, Daffodils, and Narcissus, we invested today in a 11/2" variety for the smaller bulbs that I have usually dug in by hand. "Invested" is a key word – about $30.00 a piece. They attach to your drill, so they can be used anywhere you can stretch an outdoor extension cord. (The rechargeable battery drills may run out of power quickly with such a draw on their energy.)

The second key is to cut out the bottom out of a 7 – 8" diameter plastic pot. Center the pot over the spot where you want to drill. Hold the pot with one hand and the drill with the other. That way the dirt stays close to the hole for easy closure after sprinkling in some bulb toner. Ideally, two people plant together, so that the job goes quickly. What used to be a laborious process, using a hand-held short corer or a larger pole variety, can now be done quickly, efficiently, and relatively painlessly. It's all in the auger!

What tasks that you do are best done by two? If "best done by two" applies, do you confer with the other? In advance?

What tools make your life simpler and do not diminish quality?

When you have become more efficient, do you plant more bulbs? If not, my husband would like you to teach me that lesson of restraint!

If this lesson applies to the rest of your life, what are the positives and what are the negatives?

All I Want for Christmas...

My mother, at age 85 or so, announced her request for Christmas – a chain saw! Originally 5'5", but then close to 5 feet and 100 pounds, this wacky woman wanted a chain saw to use in her Tucson garden. One wonders exactly what she had in mind... Mesquite and other small dead trees that could be turned into firewood for her beehive fireplace? We halfway contemplated sending her a toy version... but then thought, maybe I should just go to visit instead.

Mom always loved her garden tools. I have many of her trowels, watering nozzles, botanical arrangement shears, "frogs," and watering cans. One particular watering can, that she used when cultivating a garden up the hill away from their summer apartment in Albany, New York, has braided cotton strips around the metal handle – it was obviously cutting into her hand as she carried water from the spigot by the building. She had sought special permission to plant tomatoes, etc. and then hand-watered.

Gardening is a passion, not governed by age, common sense, or environment. Thank heavens for that. Certainly, Mom's passion for gardening was a multi-generational gift. We three girls and our children have got the gardening DNA in our genes. (I married into similar DNA, so it was a marriage made in garden heaven.)

What irrational gifts have you wished for?

What tools have you coveted for your garden? Life?

What tools have you treasured for your garden? Life?

While tools are important, what is more important?

Aprons as Armor

A sister gardener, who is also an incredible textile artist, gave me some heavy beige canvas to make gardening aprons. You know the style, with adjustable neck strap and pockets for tools, gloves, and tissues. Mine more likely holds a pen and note pad to catch the fleeting visions and "to do's!" I just happened to have some beige heavy-duty cotton with a black motif of garden tools to enhance these creations... a labor for our church bazaar, which attracts many gardeners – male and female.

When I am out snipping flowers and greens along my corner in Mystic, I think my apron sends the message that I work here – I am not just filching a bouquet from what some might think is a public space. You would be surprised... a friend whose husband was president of a local college brought bundles of Hydrangeas to the office one day, saying that she wanted to share them with co-workers before "poachers" cleaned off her bushes "like last year!"

Do gardeners wear aprons any more? Some garden clubs have their own with logos – worn for the down and dirty, but also when hosting garden tours. Just like painters who have their favorite smocks and chefs with their preferred style of coverage, serious gardeners know the benefits of their occupation-specific uniform.

What "uniform" have you adopted
for your botanical world?
professional world?

Is it purely functional?

Purely symbolic?

A mix?

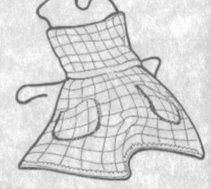

Disinfect Your Tools, Containers, and Gloves

When we work with plantings that have been infested (often true when we volunteer), we need to be conscientious about cleaning our tools, containers, and gloves so that we do not spread the infestation to our own gardens. A bleach spray helps the first two, and a thorough washing of gloves with bleach does the latter.

Infestations of all sorts occur and we may encounter them when we least expect them. Once we identify them, our response needs to be the same: to eradicate (if possible) and to ensure that we do not spread them. For example, mulch on our church landscaping brought us tuberous vines that are exceedingly difficult to eradicate. Rather than put that debris in our town brush pile, I put it in paper bags that will be incinerated.

In our places of business and significant volunteer activity, we are loath to admit that we may have insidious infestations at work (not just computer viruses).

How do we determine if they are nefarious?

If they are, how do we combat them?

How do we prevent further contagion?

If the treatment injures some of the host plants, what choices can we make for contagion-resistant plants? people?

131

Function-Discrete Areas

A writing-desk, a table with no drawers, appeared in my home decorating magazine this month, and I wondered how many people really have such a clean-topped surface unfettered by a laptop, a clock, etc. Today, many family members' desks have been communalized in the family room, where everyone has access (and supervision). I wonder if the few remaining private spaces are the sewing room, workshop, and potting shed? Function-discrete, these areas attract only those who are passionate about their hobbies.

My husband and I are fortunate enough to have all three of these spaces. Obviously, the sewing room and workshop usually draw us separately. But, we share the potting shed – a long space off of our attached double garage. Filled with shelves hosting pots, plastic containers for deadheads, garden supplies, a triple stainless steel sink (a cast-off from a local church remodeling years ago), recycling tubs, and counter space, this is in year-round use. My husband plants his vegetable starts in the spring there and we dry seed pods from Mesclun, Liatris, and Ligularia from an overhead drying rack. Off-season, it also houses boxes of publications for the Community Coalition for Children until I can disseminate them to members for distribution. At holiday time, it holds buckets of evergreens and berries, awaiting use in bouquets and fireplace mantel arrangements. A luxury? Yes! Not handsome, but functional, it helps us be who we are.

Do you have nooks and niches that serve your special interests?

By being able to keep them "set-up," are you more likely to involve yourself frequently?

How could lessons learned here impact your workplace?

132

CHALLENGES...

What Grows Here?

When my husband was ordered to the brand new submarine base at Kings Bay, Georgia, I wondered what would grow there (and would I grow there?). Located in the far southeastern corner of the state, it had been an Army depot long-inhabited by Fox Squirrels, Armadillos, Great Blue Herons, and Snakes both poisonous and "benign." Few structures had been built, but some colonial era ruins and Native American burial sites remained.

On my walks out the back roads with our Black Labrador, I encountered all of the above inhabitants, plus fossils dredged up in preparation for the submarines – fossils from 25 million years before now lay on the sand-covered roads. Palmettos filled the underbrush. Snakes lurked beneath the berry bushes, hoping to have careless birds for lunch. Crawfish filled the sloughs by the sides of the roads – hence, the arrival of the Great Blue Herons.

I soon found myself involved in two intriguing projects. One, a book called *Let's Go Fly a Kite: Activities for Kids in NE Florida and SE Georgia*, researched by members of the Kings Bay Officers' Wives' Club, focused on all of the remarkable things families could do in the region. The other, *Choosing the Right Plants for SE Georgia and NE Florida*, was the brainchild of members of the Harbour Town Garden Club in St. Marys. They wanted to help the new people who were moving in droves into their special environment to understand what plantings would thrive around their new houses. The Camden County Agricultural Extension Service was an additional invaluable resource for both of these books, for which I served as editor and publisher.

Did I grow and thrive? You bet I did!

Were others swept into the projects with growth opportunities as well?

Did we all learn about the challenges of marketing, having to find courage to go on regional radio and television programs, as far away as Jacksonville?

Did we relish not only our own products, but also the camaraderie and the enriched environments for families?

We found common bonds with which to bridge the old and the new, the military and the civilian communities, and we built skills that would be useful to us throughout our lives. Sometimes we flourish when we least expect to.

Have you ever found yourself in a new/challenging environment?

Were you able to find collaborative companions?

Were you able to make a difference (for yourself and others)?

Who's Been in My Yard?

All sorts of creatures inhabit or pass through our yards. Visible reminders range from nibbled leaves (the Slugs' and Grasshoppers' lunch), the scat from Geese, the Great Blue Heron, and neighborhood Dogs and Cats, and the feathers of song birds that indicate that a Falcon, Hawk, or Cat has been catching prey. Deer scat and nibbled Hosta leaves make clear that large animals visit our pond terraces. These events usually happen out of earshot or eyesight, so coming upon the evidence is always a little startling and a reminder that our land belongs to us in name only.

Seagulls leave blue Mussel shells. Otters leave fresh water Clamshells near our dock. Fishermen leave bobbers dangling in the bushes that overhang the pond – usually the result of early morning forays. My two grandsons have discovered the magically productive source for Worms for fishing – the drain outside our pond room door. They live there peacefully except for one week in August each year.

Do others invade our lives?

Do we notice?

Can we co-exist with others who place no demands on us?

What impact do these shadow "neighbors" have on us?

Sometimes after snow has fallen, we discover human footprints in our yard. Who was it? What were they thinking? I find it unnerving that unknown people pass through our corner Mystic property (a shortcut?). The police recommend keeping a camera handy...

No Man Is an Island

While we gardeners often consider ourselves masters of all we survey, the truth is that we are not in control. Whatever our neighbors plant often comes our way, and vice versa – not out of any desire to disrupt anyone else's plan. Creatures and wind have a way of sharing the wealth with the neighborhood.

At both the pond and in Mystic, we have neighbors with Bittersweet and Poison Ivy. The birds make sure that we have a chance to remove the starts which they have deposited in their scat while sitting in our trees. Once I told my story to a new neighbor who did not recognize the vine that had inveigled its way into a huge Burning Bush on his property, he arranged to have it eradicated. My story was that I sat for hours on my gardening stool under my Pine alleè, using surgical gloves to remove the carpet of Poison Ivy starts. Bless him!

Other "gifts" come our way: Squirrel-borne nuts and the resulting tree starts; and wind-borne dried Catalpa pods from a nearby tree (I keep wondering if I couldn't spray them gold and turn them into some kind of exciting holiday decoration or wreath — no success on that front yet). And we do our share of "giving" – Burning Bush starts and Maple saplings, not to mention Pine cones and invasive Ivy and Pachysandra. So, our island tides wash both directions.

What beneficent and maleficent landscape gifts have you received?

Ditto in your life?

Can we be more mindful of how we cross boundaries, both horticultural and psychological?

Are there spiritual equivalents?

Transplanting

I find it practically impossible to just throw away plants when I must thin them out. Some of my glorious Hostas require notes to myself in my calendar to divide in the early spring. They can then be shared with family or put in at the pond where terraces are eager for showy, low maintenance plants.

Friends now have their own burgeoning supplies of perennial Ageratum, Evening Primroses, and Ivy that will fill the shadiest grove. Most settings to which I transfer my excess are not optimum growing conditions. I know that they will struggle to survive, but I want to give them a chance. I recognize that that is a choice I make – not to make a clean break and just clear them out.

What things/activities do you simply toss away?

What things/activities do you attempt to share with family, friends, or worthwhile causes?

What things/activities are you loath to clear out entirely?

Do relationships also fall in this category?

What motivations do you notice at play in these decisions? (e.g., Procrastination? Fear of loss? Reluctance to cut all ties to memories or connections in certain domains?)

Don't Move Once Established

The Trout Lily comes with two attributes: "reliable bloomer" and "don't move once established." Because I am a military daughter and wife, the two seem inextricably combined sometimes. In my experience with my own children and those of others, I have noted that frequent relocations can be difficult for those who are "slow to warm up." Others thrive upon new opportunities and settings.

There are plants and folks who cannot thrive when relocated. They are generally those for whom a deep taproot is requisite. But there can be variations on the theme, as Trout Lilies do not fit that description. So, the tradeoff becomes stability in order to be a "reliable bloomer." As gardeners and community leaders, we are always looking for the right balance in our culture (horticulture and otherwise).

How do you choose the stock for your gardens on the reliability-relocatability scale?

How do you select your volunteers/employees on the same scale?

Which plants/people/positions should fall in the "don't move" category because of their characteristics and/or their responsibilities?

Which plants/people/positions could blossom under scenarios in which there is mobility?

Which other relationships/friendships do/do not survive the move?

I have transplanted many of my staple perennials from Connecticut to Virginia and back, so know that they can withstand the mobility, if given enough time, nutrients, and TLC (tender loving care). And so can I.

Weeds — Random Acts of Unkindness

Where do all of the clover plants, grasses, and other pernicious weeds come from? How do they zero in on my garden beds? In the natural world there are no effective barriers to seed transmissions. Birds consume and transport them, as do some insects. And this year, with our huge rainfalls in early July, water sheeting off the neighbors' back yards brought both moisture and seeds. The result is a plague of overnight giants. Nothing I treasure would ever grow that fast or profusely!

So, too, in our human world. Although we may think we have built successful barriers to the ills of the world and the ill-mannered we wish to avoid, they find a way to intrude upon us.

What ills of the world have invaded your terrain?

What strategies will you use to keep them at bay?

What ill-mannered people have crossed your path?

How do you intend to deal with them? How will you preclude them from rooting and spreading in your garden?

* It is fitting that the genesis of the Judeo-Christian tradition is in the Garden of Eden – both a place of delight and the iconic challenge of good and evil.

Tenacity —
a Weed's Middle Name

Thou art nothing if not tenacious, oh weeds that infest my pond bank. Indeed, you weeds possess a number of maddening traits. You spread on endless thin spidery roots, running just under the surface of the worst soil possible. You love being disturbed. You come back even more numerous than before my frustrated attempts to pull you out. You blossom and go to seed early in the season, often by mid-June, so you beat the competition by a long shot. Garden club friends agree that the only way to minimize Sorrel's impact (you notice that I did not say "eradicate") is to persist in pulling you out. So, I must match your tenacity. It is an uneven match!

My wrist is sore, my fingernails are filthy (even with gloves), and my knee hurts! This is the result of three hours of Sheep Sorrel removal on my pond bank, so that last year's new Hostas stand a chance of survival. And I haven't put a dent in this year's blooming Sorrel population.

Removing Sheep Sorrel is much like removing all of the pernicious little habits of our lives. Can you think of any that fit this category?

Do you combat any conditions or species that take on a magnitude of their own in the good vs. evil domain?

Will our determination and tenacity serve us in good stead for more important challenges in the rest of our life? (I certainly do hope so!)

Early Spring Pestilents

No, you didn't misread the spelling – those are the pests who combine to make pestilence! Namely: Maple tree starts, Touch-Me-Nots, and Roses of Sharon. On this third week in April, I am pulling out all of these starts. I must have more than 100 Touch-Me-Nots in my dog's backyard alone – along the border with my neighbor where the soil is usually moist. Even though one of its attributes is that the succulent stem contains a watery juice which soothes the itching of Poison Ivy, according to my favorite little book, *Wildflowers of Connecticut*, by Dr. John E. Klimas, Jr. (published for Audubon Society, State of CT, 1968), it is an ungainly, tall invader. The same area, plus the whole grassy area in the yard, sports Rose of Sharon starts. I know that many cherish this woody bush, but it is not one of my favorites.

In my main Mystic garden, I am busily weeding out all of the invasive Bellflowers that I bought from a catalog nursery some years ago (the ones with the whitish-pink blossoms) with no forewarning that they were <u>big time invasive</u> – they would take over your entire garden and squeeze out everything else! Early spring with moist soil is the optimum time to remove them, but one should not stand on the soil – so reaching stretches some muscles that will catch up with me tomorrow.

One woman's pests are another's pleasures. Some of you may treasure the plants mentioned above. I know that children love to pinch the blossoms of the Touch-Me-Nots (okay at the pond in some wild areas, but not in my civilized back yard). And Roses of Sharon will be found in historic garden plans – but they should come with warning tags saying that their seeds spread like crazy.

Don't we wish that all invasive species would come with warning tags?

Human specimens as well as botanical species?

What kind of discipline does it take to remove them when they are most vulnerable and easily removed?

How much forewarning and awareness are required to recognize these pests? Are some just personal preference and do others fall into a more generally recognized domain?

Who are your Touch-Me-Nots and Roses of Sharon?

When is it enough that they bother you vs. the rest of the world?

WARNING - INVASIVE

Foolish Mistake

Late last fall, as I was cleaning up the patio beds at the pond so I could plant a bunch of Spanish Bells, I succumbed to weariness. So, I put the bulbs in the potting shed, planning to return in the next couple of days to finish my tasks.

Foolish... I should have put them in the refrigerator vegetable bin. Instead, they froze in the shed. I felt mad with myself – now I would forfeit all of their happy blossoms come spring. Wasteful...

Have you made similar mistakes?

To what do you attribute them?

Why do we dwell on our mistakes vs. our successes?

It has been said that we need ten compliments or successes to counter-balance one slight or negative remark. Could we experience grace by realizing that we are human? That we have failed, but can be forgiven? Are we harder on ourselves than anyone else would be? Why?

Jumping Junipers!

What a mistake I made yesterday... I trimmed the Juniper bushes at the end of the Mystic driveway in bare arms and legs! Today my skin is full of red scratches and pinpricks. Who knew that leaning into those bushes to use my big trimmers would result in such a rash. I did have gloves on!

How like life. I anticipated muscle soreness, but not puncture wounds and allergic reactions. My desire to improve my line of sight made me unconscious of the side effects.

What incidents can you think of when the goal blinded you to the impediments? Discomforts? Ramifications?

Were the results worth it in hindsight? Botanically? Professionally? Personally?

What would you do differently next time?

What kind of armor might you need? Armor can be physical, emotional, and philosophical/spiritual.

I know for sure that I will wear heavy trousers and a significant jacket.... next time. My professional Junipers caused me to don regulatory armor in order to champion the causes and cases that brought scratches and punctures...

Things That Go Hop in Your Garden

No, not the proverbial "thump in the middle of the night!" These hoppers can be benign or not so. Benign are the little brown speckled Toads who lurk under the Pachysandra or in the rotting tree trunk bases, amazingly camouflaged. They eat lots of insects and spiders, and are startled when the watering spray hits them.

The Bullfrogs enjoy our pond shoreline, especially where we leave their favorite murk of rotting leaves and branches (which are not so popular with kayakers and canoeists as they launch from an adjacent area). Sounding like drumming timpani, they make amorous antiphonal choruses across the pond – a wondrous accompaniment to evenings on the porch.

Grasshoppers are a bane. They munch avariciously on favorite leaves (like the deep purple Elephant Ears and Shasta Daisies). When caught, they make great fish food as they energetically breast stroke across the surface of the pond. Praying Mantises are also hoppers. While fiercely unattractive, almost primeval (prime evil!) in appearance and habit (she eats her mate), they do consume a lot of the bad bugs in the garden. Lessons for life?

Know your hoppers… friend or foe? How do you attract your friends? What conditions are friendly to your foes?

In spite of Dr. Albert Schweitzer's philosophy of not stepping on an insect if it is not doing you harm, we need to stomp on Grasshoppers (c.f., the plague of Locusts) and Cockroaches (just visit the Smithsonian Institution's display of their rate of reproduction!). Who are some Grasshoppers you know?

What multiplies at the same rate as Cockroaches? Rumors? Frivolous emails? Catalogs in your mailbox? Phone calls at dinnertime?

Sweet Woodruff

To achieve a shaded bank of Sweet Woodruff requires years of patience and watering while the little web of roots slowly builds into a hidden mat. Perseverance is rewarded with little umbrella-like leaf whorls and dancing white blossoms in spring.

I received my start from a good friend who had Sweet Woodruff creeping into her gravel driveway. I was surprised how much care it took to really get a good hold on my pond bank, albeit the soil there is terrible. If I failed to be attentive in watering during dry spells, I risked my entire previous investment.

Some plants are really high maintenance, especially at the beginning. Do you have any that fit this category?

How is this like friendships?

In what ways is this high maintenance factor similar to other endeavors?

How do we weigh the choice to initiate such an undertaking? Do we realize the commitment at the beginning, or do we learn through experience?

*Sweet Woodruff is listed in some horticultural encyclopedias as Bedstraw – I bet there's an interesting history there!

148

The Dichotomy of Acorns

Yes, the Deer and Squirrels love them. But, they fall on the various stairs and paths at the pond and are trip hazards. Even more than that, if left undisturbed on the gravel driveway or under leaves on the banks, they require pulling out in the spring. What is the balance of nature here?

In a year when nuts of all sorts are plentiful, I presume that enough fall to feed the beasts and I can remove what I come across as I clear paths and rake the yard. In lean years, I might put a stash in the ground-level birdbath and leave some on the rock walls of the terraces.

Acorns are symbolic of food sources in our yard. Other similar challenges are nuts, tree seedpods, and Maple seeds. If they are still in our landscape after the winter is over, they start new trees ... the sprouts sometimes require removal with pliers! War is now declared!

What other natural food chain issues do we encounter in our gardens and yards?

What human food chain issues do we encounter? Are you over-supplied with Zucchini, Tomatoes, or Cucumbers? Ask your local social services agencies and food banks if they will accept fresh vegetables. Many are pleased to be able to provide more than canned or boxed goods.

What else do you have too much of? Yard goods? Office supplies? Bed linens for sizes you no longer use? Call the above-mentioned social service agencies, plus churches and women's clubs (the latter often run rummage sales and thrift shops).

As with all issues that require a balance between supply and demand, the answers are complicated... especially so if we look for humane or environmentally appropriate answers.

Too Much of a
Good Thing

When we need rain or sunshine, we rarely consider what problems would result if we got too much of what we wished for. Our country has been plagued with too much rain in some areas and too little in others. Obviously, there is a need for a balance in order for gardens and lives to thrive.

What are other things that are good in proper doses?

Food?

Exercise?

Wealth?

Friendships?

Leisure time?

Travel?

Work?

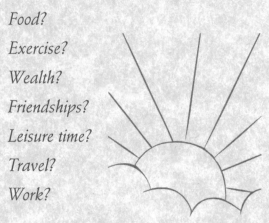

There are +/- sides to each of these experiences. Our lifelong task is to find a balance – not on any one day or in any one year, but over our lifespan. We can control some aspects of these challenges; but, some are beyond our control, such as rain and sunshine. For those, our role is damage prevention and cleanup.

Admitting to forces beyond our personal or collective control is a wise perspective and a balm for sin-sick souls. But, it does not relieve us of responsibility for prevention or intervention.

Rain

"Into every life….."

We rarely see our reported regional rain index high enough to match the newspaper's average monthly/annual rainfall report. We seem always to be behind.

With two extensive properties to water, we delight in every drop that comes our way. But, we are also amazed at the differential between two sites only 15 minutes away from each other. The micro-environmental systems are amazingly different. Because we go between these two systems almost daily in gardening seasons, we are keenly aware of the idiosyncrasies of each. We check our rain gauge results daily.

Are we as aware economically, culturally, educationally, and socially of the micro-environments in our region?

What could rain be the metaphor for in your community? Funding, taxes, benefits of all sorts?

How careful is your region with its natural resources, including water?

For you personally, what does rain constitute? What kind of gauge do you use and how frequently do you monitor it? Is the measure a purely personal one or is it referenced against some external meter? (e.g., the stock market?)

Hurricane Debris

For most of us living along the eastern seaboard, there will be memories of the preparations for, the survival of, and the cleanup from Hurricane (Tropical Storm) Irene – an extremely broad event in 2011.

What storms have you escaped relatively unscathed in your garden? your personal life? your professional life?

What role did preparedness play on your part? on the part of others?

How did the fear factor affect you for yourself? for loved ones? for pets?

How did the aftermath affect future choices? Have you been surprised by the fallout?

What real and metaphorical debris did you have to clean up? What were the characteristics of your "new normal?"

I, for one, vow to plant smaller trees whose scope does not imperil our structures. Will I cut the surviving giants? Our arborist recommends against their removal, as they actually buffer each other and the Mystic house...

Over-Exposure

Botanically, over-exposure can have two meanings: 1) a plant gets too much sun each day; and 2) a specimen plant that would be an intriguing solo accent is overwhelming in the design if too many are used. On one garden tour in our region, one yard showcased dozens of different Clematis plants, each one spectacular by itself, but en masse lost impact. (The sum was less than its parts.)

This can be true in human relationships as well.

Are there domains in which our young people receive too much exposure too soon in their development?

In your personal life, do you know folks with whom you can interface frequently and still find them "comfortable" and refreshing to be around? ditto in your professional life?

On the other hand, are there those in both your personal and professional life who are best in small doses? no doses?

How do you choreograph these brief encounters?

Rather than charging yourself with being manipulative of these contacts, reframe your strategies as self-protective. We must, in the final analysis, be arbiters of our own safety (be that physical, fiscal, emotional, or spiritual). There are some people who are not good for our well-being.

Snow Casts

As I worked today at carefully removing the icy snow casts that have covered my Blue Prince Holly bushes, I mused about how similar they were to the casts we wear for broken limbs... they must be carefully removed so as not to do further damage. With enough warmth, the Blue Prince limbs will slowly resume their former shape by reaching toward the sun. So, too, will our limbs resume their shape and function when their muscles have reached and flexed.

Our mind and soul can regain their elasticity after being bound in sorrow and gloom. Once freed from their cast of sadness, they can slowly recover, and perhaps become even stronger. When we talk of being heart-broken, we wish there were a "cast" to help us mend. However, our heart, like some of our bones, simply cannot be set. Cradled in a sling, it must mend on its own, with time being a major component in the cure.

Have your gardens revived from icy onslaughts?

Have your limbs recuperated?

Has your intellect survived periods of deprivation and dysfunction?

Has your heart mended?

Has your soul returned to song?

Have you helped to remove others' casts?

Crisis Management

Questions to garden experts often focus on what to do with areas that have standing or running water at the beginning of the spring. And the wise answer usually involves learning to find the right plants for those wet spots rather than trying to fight Mother Nature. That will bring sustainability vs. an annual battle to make the sites conform to the gardeners' wishes.

As a former teacher and parent, I hear the echo of trying to mold children into the forms we adults desire rather than helping them be masters of their fate… and then delighting in the results.

The Chinese figure for "Crisis" is actually a combination of the characters for "Disaster" and "Opportunity." What crises have you resolved in your garden?

危 機

What crises have you resolved in your life?

When did the resolution involve finding the right plant for the troublesome conditions?

When did your life challenges involve seeking serendipitous solutions?

I cannot resist a personal example of the latter. Teaching at the junior high and high school levels gave me a great deal of pleasure and a sense of accomplishment. By the time we had moved to several different locations, however, I found that school systems preferred not to hire folks with a master's degree and five years of teaching. By great good fortune, I began writing articles for magazines distributed to military families worldwide, and serving this population in a variety of professional ways became my life's work – my niche became less local and less vulnerable to changes in the landscape.

The Climate Is Changing

For years, gardeners and nurserymen relied on the multi-zone USDA chart to determine what could or could not survive in general geographic environments. However, we are now more aware than ever that both macro- and micro-environments have been modifying... maybe cyclically or permanently.

When I was told 20 years ago that Redbud trees could not thrive in Southeastern Connecticut, I was puzzled because they flourished on the Smith College campus in Northampton, Massachusetts – an hour and a half north of us and in a notorious snow belt. I bought a Redbud near Fort Detrick, Maryland and transported it home in my car. It thrives!

For two decades, I have been rooting Aucuba, a yellow-spotted broadleaf evergreen also known as Japanese Laurel, and have been planting it on both Connecticut properties. I first received cuttings from my mother-in-law in Arlington, Virginia. It has not been available in local nurseries until this past year, and I have seen only one bush on a local garden tour. My bushes have grown so prolifically that I have to be inventive in giving the rooted clippings away.

What gardening changes have you noted?

What changes in the workplace do you attribute to climate change? Social climate? Economic climate? Intellectual/aesthetic climate?

What is the critical mass needed for acceptance of these changes?

What does "cutting edge" mean to you? Have you been on it?

P.S. Sixteen years later, I was able to buy a Redbud tree locally in Connecticut and it is flourishing at the pond.

Location[3]

The old real estate adage, "Location, Location, Location," is true for gardeners in both the macro and micro sense. Micro-environments include sun and shade, humidity vs. aridity, volcanic or humus soils, and good drainage vs. a substrata of clay. One area in my Mystic garden worries me each winter. It is an extension of the original garden and required the excavation of a large rock. Lots of mulch and humus were poured in, but it continues to be the lowest point and tends to ice over in the winter. But, guess what? My deep purple Lobelia, part of the Cardinal Flower family, absolutely loves it because it wants wet feet. Over the last two years, it has spread delightfully.

People are the same way. To some degree we can choose our macro- and micro-environments.

On the hardiness charts, which zone is your favorite? Do you migrate in some seasons? Do you relish experiencing all four seasons?

Are you sensitive to the diminished sunshine in the winter?

Do you prefer urban or rural settings?

Do you like getting your feet wet?

Do you thrive best with space around you or do you like neighbors and co-workers close by?

Those who can work anywhere due to electronic interface can truly select an environment in which they thrive.

Drought Indicators

Military preparedness has long focused on early warning indicators. Gardeners do likewise. We know that the drying out of Sensitive Ferns at any time in the year is a precursor to other plants being thirsty. Pachysandra gets the wilts. In the fall, Burning Bush is a prime indicator when things are dry and seasonal foliage color is on its way. When Evening Primrose leaves turn red before fall, they signal a dearth of water.

Wouldn't it be wonderful if we had such obvious signs of deficits or changing conditions in our personal and business lives?

While a barometer measures air pressure, predicting a change in the weather, what are your garden predictors?

What are your personal predictors? Signs of distress?

What are the predictors in your business and major volunteer settings?

Do you heed these signs and what do you do about them? Having not been raised in areas prone to drought, I was astonished to learn from Texas friends that their house foundations begin to crumble in protracted drought conditions. This has poignant personal implications...

We have learned that we experience distress on the national level as well. Think about the variety of indicators that have been touted as measures of the weakening (or improving) economy over the last few years.

Poisonous Beauties

What a surprise to learn recently that Monkshood is toxic to the extent that when handling or pruning it, one should avoid getting any juice from the plant near our mouth or an open wound. Obviously, the answer is to wear gloves, preferably the latex-dipped variety that can be washed off easily afterwards.

Most of us know that Poinsettias and Bittersweet berries are poisonous to humans. Nightshade (berries) and Pokeberry (berries and roots) fall in the same category. Poison Ivy and Sumac are notorious for their punishment of the unwary.

You probably know individuals who exemplify this phenomenon as well. Attractive from afar, they are dangerous in proximity. How often have you noted someone's achievements, but commented, "I'd hate to work for her (or him)?" Unfortunately, most folks do not share forewarnings about people as readily as they would share the traits of dangerous flora.

What other plants fall in the "admire, but do not touch" category?

What people should be treated with the same caution?

What traits do they have in common?

Why are we loath to identify them for what they are?

159

Bumps, Bruises, and Bites

My arms and legs bear evidence of my hard labor in the garden. Hauling barrels of debris and brush leaves me with purple legacies that are evidence of my determination. "Badges of honor" is my new name for the body tattoos from my garden passions. All of us who use the "baby aspirin" daily know that we are vulnerable to casual bruising. How did I get that? I don't remember bumping myself that hard...

Does that mean that we will stop our usual gardening regimens?

When I was conquering nasty weeds on my pond bank, a spider found his way into my shoe leaving a nasty hard knot on my toe later that night. Can I avoid all pests?

Preventive bug spray is a daily routine – anti-mosquito and Lyme ticks – it is just smart. Can I prevent all bumps, bruises, and bites?

Do these visible results of our risky gardening behaviors diminish our pleasure? Vanity has no place in a gardener's first-aid kit.

Workplace and family encounters bring their own variations of bumps, bruises, and bites. How do we prevent and/or treat those?

Crabgrass

Have you noticed that when rainfall is below the annual average, your lawn and ground covers begin to wilt? You are tempted to water the lawn, but the Crabgrass is already thriving. What a bane! It isn't fair!

Such is nature – Mother and otherwise. The bad/evil seem to flourish under adverse conditions. There is one consolation: it is easier to spot the insurgents and, if you have the fortitude, to extricate them one by one. Your ground cover should get special treatment, but your grass will survive without watering in most situations.

Have you weathered a shortage of rainfall lately? What lessons did you learn?

Have you seen the Crabgrass phenomenon in your workplace?

In your personal life, have you been able to pluck the Crabgrass when it becomes obvious in a crisis? Relationships often fall in this category.

In tight economic times, have you seen the Crabgrass phenomenon at work in a variety of ways, on both personal and national levels?

Weeding = Time for Meditation

While many see weeding as a chore, I often welcome the quiet pensive time. Apart from our garden beds, we also have a gravel driveway and parking area at the pond that threatens to turn into a "garden" if I do not pay attention. Especially after heavy rains, which drain our neighbors' yards down the driveway, we get Dandelions, Mullein, and Heal-All. My own wild gardens spread their Violets and Wild Geraniums. And, of course, the native New England Asters would love to increase their reach.

Pesticides and herbicides are out of the question as the whole area drains into Long Pond. So, weeding becomes quiet time for the mind and soul while the fingers work. Surgical gloves and cast-off dental tools help extricate those tiny starts. I am rewarded periodically with seedlings of Lungwort and False Solomon's Seal that are progeny of the small raised garden beds in the parking area. They get new homes.

Many of life's tasks are potentially boring, so the answer is to use the time for intensely personal introspection, for which we rarely carve out enough time.

What tasks or hobbies fill this niche for you? Gardening? Other?

What examples can you give of highly productive outcomes?

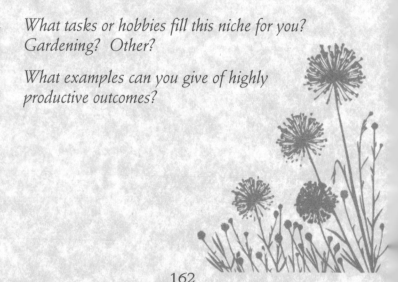

Lemonade

On this snowy morning, the front walk in Mystic is lined with branches cut from the Hawthorn tree. My husband was able to salvage one strong trunk system, but the rest had split under the weight of the heavy snowfall and were resting dangerously on nearby bushes. So, we now have brush cover for birds who are darting in and out with delight, feeding on the accessible berries.

A huge Pine bough is likewise partially cut up by the driveway and is providing ground level cover for wildlife. Once the snows have melted, we will chop up the various branches and cart them away.

What similar gardening experiences have given you the opportunity to make lemonade out of lemons?

What life experiences mimic this dynamic?

When we bought our dear "doll's house" in Vallejo, California, we joined a group of stucco-beam-and Mexican tile homes in what had been an orchard enclave. Among the treasures in our yard were a big Lemon bush, a Damson plum tree, and several big Cherry Plum trees. I've written elsewhere about the resulting marmalade, brandy, jam, and mash (to put over ice cream), but the best part was the "garden party" – no one was allowed to leave without filling a grocery bag full of fruit to take home – plus the recipe for the brandy!

Sharing a Garden
is Hard to Do!

I can no longer find my Lady's Mantle at the pond – a source of great delight in a shady spot near my potting shed. It has been overwhelmed by my husband's invasive Ostrich Ferns, which he protects fiercely, even though they have clearly gone beyond agreed-upon bounds.

In his vegetable garden in Mystic, he fusses that my herbs take up valuable sunny space (right at the front where I can pick them easily). Though we are both generally congenial gardeners, he owes me a new Lady's Mantle, which I will plant far away from his precious Ferns.

There are other spaces in our lives where "territories" and "tastes" conflict. What are some of yours?

Do you share your office space? Do you share your computer? printer? phone?

When do you acquiesce after due notice that your preferences have been abrogated?

When do you stand your ground?

He owes me a new
Lady's Mantle!

P.S. He bought me one
and helped me plant it.

Gardens: For Ourselves?
For Others?

Have you ever experienced the subtle (or not so subtle) put-down? In our world of gardening, this may come when a landscape designer comments that yours is a "garden of opportunity" (i.e., you plant what intrigues you vs. having a grand plan). Hint: this could be part of the marketing of services plan!

First and foremost, our gardens should give us pleasure. When most start gardening, it is for our own physical exercise and aesthetic delight. Perhaps, over time, we begin to share our gardens with others – informally at first, and then because the local garden club, historic society, or fund-raising charity has asked. Opening a garden to the public is indeed an act of charity because, in most cases, you-the-gardener will be expected to do all of the prep work and clean up. (The docents will appear to act as hostesses.)

How true this is of our lives. Hopefully, our work pleases us (not always true, but an ideal component). When what we do enters the public forum, either as paid or unpaid providers, we are subject to others' expectations.

What do you love to do? What boundaries do you draw between your private and public personae?

When these activities that you love take you into a public forum, how much of the prep work and cleanup falls to you?

Do you get to bathe in public admiration?
Does this matter to you?

Do you lose something and/or gain something in the process?

Voices on the Pond

Water carries voices of all sorts: the calls of Great Blue Herons, Kingfishers, Ospreys, Ducks, Geese, Blue Jays, Cardinals, Orioles, and Bullfrogs. Each adds his music to the antiphonal choir, as do Dogs and Cats, echoing along the pond. Humans, oblivious to the water amplification factor, add to this cacophony.

While gardening with brain waves in the Alpha zone, one hears these "conversations" amplified. Years ago we heard a barbershop quartet rehearsing on the pond, kids singing Fourth of July songs, and a lone guitarist plying his trade. These fall in the domain of "simple gifts" that bring delight.

> *Sweet wafting sounds are different from overly loud commercial music electronically amplified.*
>
> *What would you like to hear in your reverie?*
>
> *What is the agreed-upon close-up time for outdoor neighborhood parties and music?*

There is a difference between agreeable sharing and intrusion. We need to be good neighbors not only to the humans around us, but to the wonderful birds and beasts who also call our pond home. Fourth of July fireworks bring sheer terror to our Black Labrador, so we leave him home in Mystic and hope that he hears less there. We must guard our pond roofs from the flaming detritus of illegal exuberance!
Talk about intrusion!!

166

DELIGHTS...

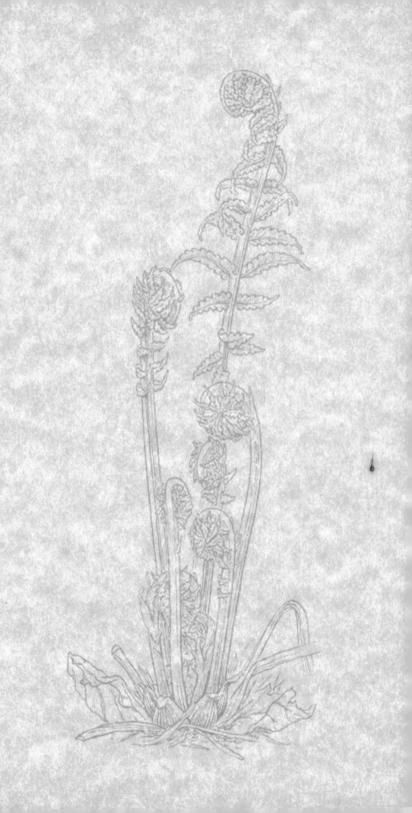

Little Delights

Spring is the time for little delights at Long Pond. The wild red with yellow Columbine emerges from the cracks in the big rocks up in the meadow. Left there by the glacier eons ago, these rocks are home to various wild berries and False Solomon's Seal, plus Indian Pipes at the base. While we have "cultivated" relatives of the Columbine in our shed bank garden, these little wild ones are especially treasured.

Likewise our blue haze of Blue-eyed Grass comes before the trees have leafed out. These tiny little gems pack a punch beyond their Lilliputian size. They ring the edges of rock steps, their yellow centers set off by their light blue petals.

Our low Phlox (*Phlox divaricata*) carpets the patio chimney beds and shows up in a few other spots as well. Some few bunches of the bright colored Creeping Phlox remain from previous owners. The small Tulips are exalting in their reds and yellows, so spring announces its glory on Long Pond with a bang, not a whimper (à la T.S. Eliot).

Sometimes small delights can bring disproportionate pleasure. What examples can you think of in your garden?

What examples can you think of in your life?

Sometimes, in our search for the big show, we miss the little wonders.

Resolve today to be a seeker of small delights.

Bewitching Witch Hazel

Thanks to the designer of our church's memorial garden, we have a glorious Witch Hazel tree *"Arnold's Promise"* that explodes in a crown of yellow in mid-March, about a week before spring arrives officially and often before the final snow of the season. It simply radiates joy. In full view from our sanctuary windows, it is an outward and visible sign of renewal, the Biblical theme for the season.

The fact that Witch Hazel bark has long been used to produce an alcoholic tonic and lotion that are good for bruises and sprains adds to its practical and metaphorical value. (In fact, our region is the historic home of significant production of Witch Hazel products. They came before the federal regulations, so are considered non-pharmaceutical remedies.)

One does have to be careful to get the right cultivar, because some have rather drab mixtures of brown and yellow blossoms. This reminds us that even within a family, botanical or otherwise, there can be variations.

Do you know people who simply radiate joy? Do you seek out their company?

Do you know folks who are like a tonic, soothing your emotional and spiritual bruises and sprains?

Would you consider planting a Witch Hazel where it could give you (and others) delight?

Our Naval medical clinic has several Witch Hazels on the bank near the entrance – wonderful metaphors for those who know their history.

Little Blue Scillas

These intensely blue midgets bring the winter landscape dancing into spring. Their star-like bloom often hangs like a little bell on a slender stem. Their delicate structure belies their visual pow! Their ability to spread from year to year is a gardener's delight. They deliver their jaunty announcement of spring and then graciously give way to the larger bulbs and perennials that follow.

There have been years when they have poked their blue heads through April snow cover, like mailmen determined not to be deterred by rain, sleet, or snow. The mailmen also bring tidings of joy.

What other early announcers of spring inhabit your yard?

Who do you know who brings you small doses of delight?

How can you give small acts of kindness and pleasure? (e.g., a thank you sent on a pretty botanical notecard? an invitation for tea and conversation for two? a picnic in a garden gazebo or on the waterfront as a respite during a day-long garden tour?)

Garden Tours with a Friend

What is so rare as a day in June... on a house and garden tour with a friend? The shared passion for gardening, plus the delight in new species and clever solutions to tricky sites are some of my all-time favorite experiences. If there are two or three friends, that is even better. Each of us notices different things and brings her own expertise. The fact that our region has so many garden clubs, master gardeners, and organizations that fund-raise by showcasing gardens means that we have a plethora of opportunities to indulge in this pleasure.

When I must go alone, I have found that my camera functions like a friend. It forces me to look more carefully and to frame my experience artfully. The double value comes when I can share the results via botanical note cards.

The same double value comes when I must attend a conference or a performance alone – by journaling what I have seen and learned, I can enhance my experience. But, having companions with whom to discuss is more fun.

What interests do you share with friends? Cooking, antiquing, shopping, or music?

Why does having a friend along triple the joy?

What shared activities could you initiate?

How could you use the "bring-a-friend" concept for events in which you are involved?

172

Can You Find?

Our church Women's Fellowship was holding our end-of year luncheon out at our pond property. Many of our members are also members of various garden clubs, so I thought it would be fun to give them permission to roam under the guise of a treasure hunt.

- Aucuba
  (hint: spotted evergreen bush)
- Beebalm (Monarda)
- Bittersweet
- Bluets
  (hint: blue star grass)
- Broom
- Chinese Dogwood
- Chives
- Evening Primroses
- False Solomon's Seal
- Fern fiddleheads
- Hawk's Eye
  (hint: orange weed!)
- Hostas
- Indian Pipes
- Lace-cap Hydrangeas
- Lady's Slippers
- Lamiastrum
  (hint: tall burgundy leaves with yellow blossoms later)
- Lily of the Valley
- Lion's Foot
- Lysimachia
  (hint: creeping yellow)
- Moss
- Mountain Laurel
- Myrtle
  (Periwinkle)

- Pearly Everlasting
- Phlox divericata
  (hint: low lavender)
- Pipsissewa
  (Striped Spearmint)
- Poppies
- Sensitive Ferns
- Sheep Sorrel
  (hint: major weed!)
- Spiderwort
- Sweet Woodruff
- Threadleaf Maple
  (Japanese)
- Tiger Lilies
- Touch-me-not
- Trailing Arbutus
- Veronica
  ("Baby Blue Eyes")
- Wild Blueberries
- Wild Columbine
  (hint: in rock pockets)
- Wild Lily of the Valley
- Wisteria
- Woodland Ferns

Other finds:

_____

_____

_____

_____

They Can Live to be 100!

When you think of Lady's Slippers, what are your adjectives? Beautiful? Rare? Protected? Hard-to-transplant? Long-lived should also be a description. They can live to be 100 years old. And while they don't bloom every year, when they do produce seeds, each plant can scatter up to 100 seeds.

You can imagine my delight upon reading these characteristics in my local newspaper, not long before our four grandchildren were due to arrive (ranging then in age from 6 – 12). They love to explore our pond acre and I was worried about the explosion of Lady's Slippers I had found where an old Hemlock had blown over in a fall storm. The tree removal team had carefully replaced the torn-out soil back on the rock it so miraculously covered. In the spring, 40 Lady's Slippers arrived! We had identified seven or eight for some years, with most blooming annually, but this was an incredible gift. The area now open to the sun and blessed with good rainfall had harbored seeds for how long?

Fearing that the children would run gaily through this treasure trove, I enlisted their help in counting them. And, I told them that because they can live to be 100 years old, their children and even their grandchildren might be able to enjoy their blooms. This year much to my husband's chagrin, I have marked individuals or clusters with white plant tags. I need a visual reminder for some of the new locations – for walking, weeding, and raking. And, for grandchildren. What a responsibility for us and a legacy for them.

What else do we leave as a legacy?

What "flowering" of ours produces the equivalent of 100 seeds?

What gift is location-specific and hard-to-transplant?

Fernaholics

It may surprise you to learn that "fernaholism" is a genetically carried obsession: it passes especially from father to son! When our son arrived from his Long Island home with empty containers and tools in the back of his truck, plus Fern seed gathering kits of his own design, I knew that the affliction had settled in big time. His father has accumulated all sorts of Ferns from friends and nurseries, and has given our son books on Ferns – a wonderful generational heritage.

We hope that he, too, will remember where and from whom he acquired his treasures. Each of the different species requires different soil, sun, and water. There are the Sensitive Ferns that spread astronomically, but disappear seasonally when there is a lack of water. There are evergreen species, visible when the snow surrounds them. The Cinnamon Ferns bring the classic fiddleheads to our garden – too precious to ever consider eating. The Ostrich Ferns, invasive but beautiful, grow in "disadvantaged" soil conditions if watered enough. They are tough to transplant, but can expand their reach in the blink of an eye.

How does each of these remind you of people you know?

> *Sensitive Ferns?*
> *Evergreen Ferns?*
> *Cinnamon Ferns?*
> *Ostrich Ferns?*

Do you share a common passion with family members or friends?

How does this common bond enrich your lives?

Begonias – Shady Treasures

Do you know people who thrive in the shadows— not wanting the limelight? Begonias are the perfect metaphor for these shy fireworks.

Blessed with shiny leaves and exuberant clumps of pink, red, yellow, and orange blossoms, they defy their shady surroundings. They remind us that "full sun" is not a requisite for achievement.

Do you know Begonias in your family?

In your workplace?

Do you value their potential?

Do you honor their desire to thrive out of the glare of the spotlight.

Scentsational

Yesterday, as I pulled up watering cans full of pond water at the north dock, I was struck by the sweet smell of Honeysuckle. While I incessantly cut out any starts that I see because they become pernicious wanderers in a hurry, I do adore their smell.

Years ago, when we first moved to Mystic (1968), the window behind our bed brought the sweet smell of Honeysuckle on humid June evenings, accompanied by the hum of what I thought was a factory – it turned out to be the hum of I-95 a mile away only somewhat muffled by a deciduous forest in between. So, I admit to relishing the scent, but not the actuality in <u>my</u> yard!

> *How does NIMBY (Not In My Back Yard) play out in your life? I fought the state connector road from I-95 into Mystic because of the impact on the village as a whole, but also NIMBY.*

> *What subtle scents do we often fail to notice? Peonies can be quite luscious.*

> *Has our over-scented world of coffees and air fresheners ruined our awareness of the natural?*

> *Are there special scents that remind you of people or places?*

Years ago, our son Michael went with me as a young teenager on a trip to Frank Lloyd Wright's "Falling Water" in Pennsylvania. Sponsored by the Smithsonian Institution, the trip fit nicely with Smithsonian evening courses he had been attending, designed for architects and students. As we got off the bus at "Falling Water," he immediately noticed the scent of the rocks, Mountain Laurel, and Moss. "It smells like Connecticut!" Today he is an architect and a gardener! No surprises there!!

Aroma Therapy –
Au Naturel

On a warm end-of-May afternoon, the Lilies of the Valley are sending forth their mirth message – a sweet delicate scent that commercial perfumes never capture. Lilacs, Roses, and Lavender also add the scent dimension to our gardens. Stargazer Lilies in an enclosed space (like a chapel or a reception room) can be almost overpowering.

Scents can transport us to places and people we have known before. They speak along neural pathways of memories that go deeper than our visually-coded remembrances. When there is a scent affiliated with an experience or emotion, we have powerful recall.

How many scents do we fail to notice because they are part of our everyday environment?

The smell of the sea? the pond?
The smell of evergreens?
The smell of freshly mown grass?
The smell of Magnolia, Spanish Moss, and mildew? familiar scents from our stints in Virginia and Georgia.

How could recognition of these scents give us momentary pleasure?

How can we intentionally tie scents to important events in our lives?

When we lived in Southern Georgia, I envied those who had Gardenia hedges – what an incredible aroma (one that the Chanel perfume has never replicated). A Gardenia hedge would be a daily reminder of my wedding bouquet.

178

Citronella Candles

One of my favorite pensive times of the day is after dinner – looking at my gardens in Mystic or enjoying the reflections on Long Pond. Some years, the big citronella candle is a necessity. Other years, it is just a delightful source of light and scent. It brings back fond memories of Girl Scout camps when we girls all packed our own bottles of citronella to combat the fierce mosquitoes in Virginia and Kansas. I even love Irish Spring soap for the same scent! It brings visions of campfires, songs, S'mores, and wonderful late night talks from our bunks. How can we use favorite scents and traditions to enhance our gardens and our lives?

Does Bee Balm enrapture you as well as the Bees and Hummingbirds?

Are there Mints that you especially enjoy?

Can you smell the Moss when it is damp?
Our meadow hillside at the pond is mostly covered in Moss, and we relish its moist scent.

What are your favorite garden scents?

In Thornton Wilder's play, "Our Town," the "Heliotrope in the moonlight" is a tender memory. Many Victorian gardens featured this highly scented purple plant, and it makes a nice patio plant to sit by. The Smithsonian Institution often features it in the Victorian gardens near the Arts and Industries Building.

179

The Vegetable Dog

Although he is not technically a "hound," our Black Labrador does hound us for green, red, orange, and yellow Peppers. And if, by chance, we are foolish enough not to keep the plants off limits to him, he will pick his own! He noses about the flower plants on the pond patio, hoping that we have hidden a Pepper or two among them. He has patience – he waits until they are ripe, and then eats every last morsel, seeds and all.

While not traditional canine fare, all of the crunchy vegetables are alluring: Celery hearts, Cucumber and Radish tips, Cabbage hearts, Carrots, and Beans. He likes them for the same reason humans do – they are fun to chew and he senses they are good for him. Would that we were so intrigued with healthy choices!

What foods do you crave?

Can you grow any of them yourself? Or pick any of them at a local farm or orchard?

What value is gained by the direct-to-your-plate process?

We had a neighbor whose agreement with her husband and two teenaged sons was that if they picked their homegrown Raspberries or Blueberries, she would make them a pie – in season that was often one pie a day! Thank heavens our Labrador doesn't pick berries!

Lightning Bugs and Stars

Sharing childhood delights with grandchildren infuses magic into our yards. "Catch a falling star and put it in your pocket, never let it fade away!" It is super to catch falling stars, but Lightning Bugs must be released before bedtime. Part of sharing the wonder is sharing the responsibility to care for wildlife.

My husband and I have gotten up on numerous occasions at home and away to see special astronomical events – Perseiad showers from our balcony in Tortola, comets and shooting stars at Sanibel Island, Florida, and the midnight skies in Grenada when our flight finally arrived. Check your local newspaper and science center news for dates. But, even without special events, our skies are marvels that we too rarely witness, and yet, our yard witnesses every night. Years ago when my husband's submarine was away, we wives got together. Just as they were about to leave, our neighbor came over and said we had to see the incredible sky – so we all lay down on the grass and had an astronomy lesson (and my husband heard about it – embellished significantly – from his sailors who were delighted that their wives were having such an experience!).

Make some popcorn and get out your binoculars and telescope. You (and your grandchildren) will be in for a real treat. You could talk about how many of the stars that we cannot even see are now thought to be able to support life....

How often we fail to look up – to enjoy the beauty of our trees and clouds.

If you are blessed with dark skies, take notice and share.

Depending on where you live, you may have night lighting interference that blocks all but the brightest stars. Does this happen in your workplace? your family?

181

Monarch of All
I Survey

In the early fall, my perennial Ageratum becomes a swath of periwinkle blue. An hour stolen at lunchtime, sitting on the path by the Mystic birdbath, allows me a hidden respite midst swirling Monarch Butterflies. They replenish in preparation for their annual pilgrimage ahead – all at eye level. I am surrounded by their quiet intensity, by their epicurean flight of delight – an awesome experience.

I feel like queen of the garden, a monarch whose subjects are all cloaked in orange, black, and white. Their aerial choreography is ephemeral – here today, and gone tomorrow. They have other places to go, sights to see, all the way to Chile or Mexico. And so, they are off, leaving their fleeting gift to the mind's eye alone.

Do you know of fleeting gifts in your garden?
in your life?

How can we be sure to witness these glorious moments –
both in the sense of seeing, but also understanding them?

Perhaps moments with your children or grandchildren
have some of the same characteristics – they change so
quickly that one must bear witness (and perhaps capture
in one's journal or album for perpetuity).

We are, in the final analysis, the monarchs of all that we personally survey. These memories are ours alone. Others' may be similar, but not the same.

182

Surprise Lilies

My first encounter with Surprise Lilies was in our new-to-us house in Arlington, Virginia, now more than 30 years ago. In the early fall, some stalks appeared out of dry earth (no leaves around) and produced gorgeous pink flowers. I marked the spot so that I could see the leaves in the spring and not overplant them. They were truly a surprise the first year and much-anticipated in succeeding years.

Now, at our pond garden, we have some that came as a bonus with a bulb order. I had forgotten that I had planted them (failed to mark them), but now eagerly await their return in mid-September each year.

What have you planted in your life's work that has returned later as a pleasant surprise?

What have you worked very hard at that didn't seem to go anywhere, and then... surprise?

Have you ever put gifts away and forgotten about them? How can you remember them?

How about little stashes of cash? jewelry?

What about photos of people and events long ago?

Recipes for Herbal Profusion

You know that time when your garden herbs have gone way beyond their bounds? It is time to use them (or lose them). It is pesto time!

Some years ago I interviewed a remarkable chef after enjoying her workshop on herbs at a local science center. My magazine served military families worldwide and was always looking for recipes that folks could use wherever they lived. This was just such a recipe. It was entirely flexible in which herbs could be incorporated and the aroma during the production alone ensured nirvana! All of those herbs being ground up in a blender and added to olive oil and Parmesan cheese made the workshop attendees' anticipation almost unbearable. Spread over slices of French bread and warmed in a portable oven, the pesto was an instantaneous success!

The same chef later worked her magic with a college club for whom I had program responsibilities. This group likes its wine, so the lecture-cum-vino was a perfect combination. I still hear raves 15 years later about "that fabulous lecture on herbs." The truth is that the wine, ability to finger each clump of herbs, and the aroma of the toasting hors d'oeuvres appealed to everyone's senses. Yes, the recipe is below.

Lifescape Pesto

One spaghetti colander full of herbs (e.g., Basil, Salad Burnet, Thyme, Sage [sparingly], Chives, Parsley [sparingly] Dill, Rosemary [sparingly], and Oregano).
You may use some or all of the above .

   1 cup olive oil
   2 TBs garlic powder
   1/2 can Parmesan cheese (approx. 1 cup)
   Optional: pine nuts (2.25 oz pkg. or 1/2 cup)

Put herbs and olive oil in blender and blend thoroughly.
Then add garlic powder and cheese. Do not blend nuts.
Keep in refrigerator or freeze.

Garden Boursin

Fill a spaghetti colander with leaves of Basil, Dill, Salad Burnet, Chives (especially Garlic Chives), Rosemary (sparingly), Oregano, and Thyme. Place in your food processor; sprinkle with olive oil to help the grinding.

In a large bowl add to the green mix:
8 oz. unsalted butter
16 oz. whipped cream cheese
1 TB salt
2 TBs garlic powder (if no garlic chives above)
½ tsp. each of Pepper, Marjoram, and Paprika

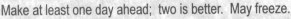

Make at least one day ahead; two is better. May freeze.
Serve on garlic rounds, Triscuits, or spread on French bread and warm.

Hints for preparing the herbs:
- Cut bunches as you are ready to work on them. Otherwise, they tend to dry quickly and look unappealing. (And you may feel overwhelmed!)
- Strip the leaves by holding the herb at almost the top (the very top tends to be tender and breaks off). Pull downward with your thumb and forefinger, dropping the leaves into your colander.
- Try to do this in the shade. The sun dries out the herbs and you!

These are time-intensive projects, but the results are creative, yummy, and "green." You can recycle a variety of jars and plastic tubs. Put the date on each jar and name creatively, as batches will taste different.

What labor-intensive garden projects pay long-range dividends? Planting Myrtle (Periwinkle) and Pachysandra comes to my mind.

What other labor-intensive projects are economical and are personal expressions?

In what other arenas does an assortment of ingredients bring incredible results?

Can you use these recipes in your workplace? Metaphorically?

185

Mozart Chutney

"Why is it called 'Mozart Chutney?'" a patron at our annual church bazaar asked. "Did Mozart make chutney?" I had to laugh and confessed that I had listened to Mozart for the four hours it took to can the chutney. And then admitted that the next slightly different batch was called "Brubeck Chutney" – same logic, but honoring his wonderful variations on traditional Christmas favorites. The recipe from an old book on canning simply called it "Mixed Fruit Chutney" – not exactly a marketing bonanza.

So, I was delighted to read in May Sarton's book, *Plant Dreaming Deep* (1968), that she often played Bach, Mozart, and Vivaldi while writing her poems. She used the same piece each time she returned to work on a specific poem. It has been fun to discover her book and creative process more than 40 years after she wrote her book.

I think that reading about gardening by those with remarkable writing skills gives me the same kind of pleasure that my mother-in-law found in cookbooks. When she had trouble sleeping at night, she would trigger her endorphins by "tasting" the recipes in her mind. A Cordon Bleu-trained cook, and a conservatory-trained pianist, she married her two passions in her kitchen listening to the classical music station. True, she could not select her music, but whiled away many mindless food prep chores in symphonic delight.

What triggers or complements your creativity?

Now that ipods make it possible to listen to music, books, sermons, etc. while you garden, have you chosen to be plugged in?

Or, do you relish the solitude and sounds of nature?

Cloudy Skies

What is your reaction to cloudy skies? It probably has something to do with scarcity of rainfall vs. a recent deluge, or a crop that needs to be harvested. Rain, especially if it is slow and can sink in, is a blessing. It saves us from endless hours of watering and decreases our water consumption and bills. Timing, of course, is everything.

When my husband and I sit on the porch at Long Pond, we can see the beginnings of a sprinkle dimpled on the pond. As a gardener, I welcome the rain. As an over-achiever, I welcome the forced indoor time – time to do the at-my-desk tasks, the planning, and reading that I have put off for a rainy day, and maybe even some musing…

What have you stored up to do on a rainy day?

Why is that gift of time so special? Does it have anything to do with the fact that it is beyond your control?

Does the rain indeed nourish us as well as our plants?

When we have not had enough rain/nourishment, what are the signs in our gardens as well as our lives?

Dancing Grasses

At the end of July, our local garden center had a 50%-off sale on small pots of Purple Fountain Grass. Three feet tall with their feathery seed heads, they brought not only their ruby stalks, but motion to our pond gardens.

By four o'clock every afternoon, there is at least a light breeze up the pond. We put a plant each in four pots on the patio that already had other plants in them (such as Black-eyed Susans and Evening Primroses), plus another six in two clumps elsewhere. Their heads nod and sway with the slightest movement of air. This enchanting choreography is almost hypnotic. They will be perennial sources of pleasure, for less than $15.00 all told.

What other plants bring motion to your garden? (Wand Plants, Lavender, Ferns, and Russian Sage come to mind.)

Some trees provide this dancing element, such as the heart-shaped leaves of Redbud.

In your personal and professional lives, what are the whimsical counterparts?

Magical Garden Sounds

A wise friend and landscape designer told me that she includes various tall grasses in her yard to buffer the noise from neighbors, but also to bring their own "swish" as breezes blow. And each of the grasses has a unique sound. Yes, she is remarkable!

My husband and I built a cathedral-ceilinged master bedroom with blown-foam insulation so we can hear the rain, sleet, and even the snow on the roof. It is like being in a cabin and hearing the whole outdoors around you – the night Owl, the early Cardinal songs, the footsteps of Crows and Seagulls as they traverse our roof to look for tasty morsels in the gutters, and Squirrels scurrying across the shingles.

In the autumn, when the lavender perennial Ageratum is in bloom, we can sit in the garden and hear the Monarch Butterflies' wings as they visit each blossom. The Goldfinches sing happy songs as the Coneflower heads are left full of seeds, just for them.

At the pond, we hear the Hummingbirds before we see them visiting our hanging pots and their red juice feeder on the open porch. We hear the constant chatter of young Cygnets and Goslings as the Swan and Goose families paddle by. The Kingfisher announces his itinerary from tree to tree. The Bullfrogs add their rich bass tones. There is so much to hear in our gardens. I choose not to hang chimes, though I enjoy them in others' yards. We have enough serenades in progress.

What discipline does it take to hear our gardens?

Should we build in the sense of sound to our garden/life? How?

189

Pond Presents

For the last couple of weeks, I have received a lovely gift almost daily: a pair of pearlescent lavender freshwater Clam shells still connected at the hinge. They signify presents and presence.

We know that we have Otters at Long Pond, as we have seen the V's on the surface as they swim away from our floating dock. An Otter must be bringing his catch to the highest step below the water line to relish his feast. So, one creature's feast is another's delight – unintended consequences!

Likewise, I receive shells throughout the yard at the pond. Seagulls drop them in order to open them. Chipmunks leave us empty acorn shells inside our pullout sofa bed – a reminder that they visit when we are not there.

What serendipitous gifts have you received?

Were they consciously given or did you happen upon them?

The Mussel shells will become part of a larger whole. They will adorn a shell mirror – a counterpoint to the seashore shells I collect. How will their use add to their value?

INSIGHTS...

S³ – Sustainable, Sustained, and Sustaining

Three gardening philosophies sound very similar and can be intertwined. The current movement toward <u>sustainable</u> gardens focuses on what to grow depending on where you live and what you grow it in (containers, raised beds, or a vegetable patch).

<u>Sustained</u> gardening focuses both on one's commitment over time and on designing to make that possible as we age and our energies flag. Sporadic maintenance does not meet the tenets of this precept.

The third takes us to a new level – gardening as an endeavor that <u>sustains</u> us (physically, aesthetically, and spiritually).

Where do you find yourself along this gardening continuum?

Is this triad equally valid in other portions of our life?

Could it be a model for businesses and non-profit organizations? (e.g., a church and its projects? a community coalition focused on open space or helping children thrive?)

It is one thing to initiate a remarkable garden or project, but it s quite another to maintain it over time with finances and energy. And, in the final analysis, does t meet the test that it sustains hose who commit themselves o it?

193

Awareness and Awe

This two-fold approach to nature brings remarkable rewards. Authors who have shared their awareness and awe include such luminaries as Henry David Thoreau, Annie Dillard, and the MacArthur fellow David Carroll (whose passion is turtles). These authors have the double gift of their intense awareness and pursuit of insights from nature, plus their ability to express their observations. Carroll has a third gift – that of drawing the creatures and environments he has monitored so carefully – sort of the Audubon of turtles.

Sitting still and blending as much as is humanly possible into a natural space enables us to use all of our senses intently. We understand on whole new levels that which we usually pass carelessly by. The result is, as Robert Grudin writes in *The Grace of Great Things: Creativity and Innovation)* (1990): *With greater insights there is prolonged wonder, not so much of being wise oneself as having stumbled into a wise world. The mind feels suddenly integrated with the power of nature and moves at nature's pace.*

> *Choose a new site in your garden each week to explore intensely.*

> *Choose a new site in your community each week or month to explore significantly.*

> *Explore actively, maybe using tools such as binoculars and a magnifier.*

> *Explore passively, simply sitting and absorbing "nature's pace."*

One of my favorite experiences with my various Girl Scout troops was to have them survey with their eye-cup magnifiers everything within the reach of their arms as they lay on their tummies – whether in the grass, on the beach, or in the woods. Talk about the "wow factor!"

Arise and
Greet the Day

Benjamin Franklin, in his *Autobiography*, encouraged us to "arise and greet the day," and then, just as intentionally, bid the day *adieu* – noting the blessings we have received (and, perhaps, giving to God the experiences that do not seem positive at the moment).

Those of us who live close to nature, whether on the beach or in a garden, know that there are several factors here. Each day that we encounter our beach or garden, we approach it in a new light – truly, because of our solar and human calendars, not to mention our emotional calendars. Some days we may find a variety of new discoveries; and on others, we are left to exult in what is "ordinary" – never really so. And, when we ask ourselves how to keep our beach/garden alive each day of our life, we must reach back to the concepts of grace, amazement, and delight.

A recent children's sermon in church reminded me that God indeed has a sense of humor. How often have we thought this as we looked at the flora and fauna around us? Some of my happiest creative moments reflect this concept – that God has provided us with metaphors that bring us the laughter of deep recognition.

Can we imagine ourselves as Emersons, Thoreaus, Dickinsons, and Dillards? Because we are…

Can we internalize Franklin's incredible discipline to ensure that we do not fail to recognize opportunities?
Do not be too hard on yourself –
he enjoyed his wine as well.

Is there value in greeting each day – intentionally?
Does that first awakening awaken?

195

Tansy Lesson

Do not let anyone tell you that you are "just an Herb" and not ready for a prime time patio pot on the edge of the pond. In full bloom, with your heavy clusters of gold on top of your fern-like leaves, you are very handsome.

The tendency to stereotype is alive and well in the garden as well as in our human world. Some tend to believe that Herbs should be kept in their place – that being a section set aside for them alone.

And yet, wise gardeners select on merit those specimens they wish to showcase. They are selected when they are at their prime for positions of honor. Prior to being in the limelight, they are nurtured so that they will achieve their potential.

What choices have you made to break stereotypes in your garden?

What unusual choices have you made in floral arrangements?

Have you had experiences in your workplace where stereotypes have been broken?

Are you conscious of the illumination that accompanies the breaking of stereotypes? And the responsibility to ensure success once you embark on this mission, because failure would be harmful to those most vulnerable.

Quarks for
Quirky People

A new book, *Soil Mates: Companion Planting for Your Vegetable Garden,* by Sara Always (2010), is cleverly named. She writes of the love matches and sordid triangles that occur in the vegetable world, making the most of human parallels and double entendres such as "my place or yours?" She also explores what each vegetable does not mix well with, and which insects are problematic for each.

Probably the closest manuals for humans are those that explore the Zodiac signs that make good pairs, or the Enneagram and Myers-Briggs profiles that are not only compatible, but also may stimulate generativity and creativity – the quarks for quirky people!

Have you tried companion planting? (e.g., Tomatoes with Basil, Cucumbers with Corn, Carrots with Onions, and Lettuce with Radishes).

Have you used flowers in your salads? (e.g., Violets, Nasturtiums, and even Marigold petals chopped for garnish).

Have you figured out what kinds of people to avoid, because they are not good for your mental health?

Have you learned what kinds of people to seek out because they help you "be all you can be?"

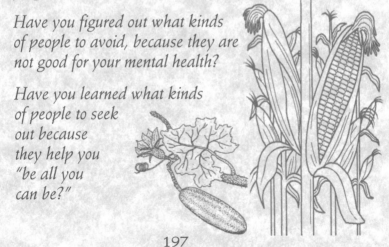

Pockets of Rockets

In mid-May, pockets of Yellow Rockets appear along our roadway margins. From afar, they look like Stock or Snapdragons, but they are more delicate (and they are a "weed" in the Mustard family).

Chicory sprouts its glorious blue blossoms in tandem with Queen Anne's Lace. If you wanted to transplant or use these flowers in an arrangement, you would quickly learn how fragile these tough "weeds" are.

So, too, on a recent trip to Beaufort, North Carolina, many of us tourists wished that we could have the bright pink Oxalis in our gardens that we saw filling yards in mid-May. Much like the Blue-eyed Grass in northern climes, they are showy early and then decline as lawns are mowed.

Beauty is in the eye of the beholder. Is a pedigree necessary to be accepted?

Could placement play a role? Do you have meadow or wild areas in your yard? In your life?

Years ago, I made a multi-tiered centerpiece of various herbs and Yellow Rocket. Everyone was challenged to identify the species. The winner got the Yellow Rocket!

What variations on this "centerpiece" could you use symbolically?

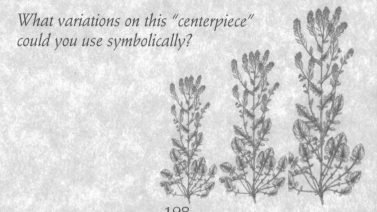

Buying Bulbs = Investment Philosophy

Just as our stockbrokers talk degrees of risk, growth, and performance (dividends/income), we need to consider our bulb purchases in the same vein. The little hybrid Tulips are indeed perennial. While small, their color and shapes add magic to our pond patio garden where they are warmed by a stone retaining wall and the house foundations. Of course, hardware cloth screens must be laid over them all winter to prevent Squirrels from consuming them – their shallow depth makes them vulnerable.

The endless varieties of Daffodils pay perennial dividends. They even multiply, much like stocks that split (don't you love those?). Hyacinths are perennial, but they do not seem to multiply. So, they are like bonds – safe, sure investments with a specified payback. Tulips are the wild cards. The flamboyant species are truly annuals – the Parrots, Rembrandts and, my new favorites, the Monsellas (red and yellow ripples of delight). They are the fast growth/little-or-no dividend stocks. The tall hybrid single color Tulips that are supposed to be perennial have not proved to be so in my garden. They would be the equivalent of a stock that promised good dividends and then tanked. (I've owned a few of those!)

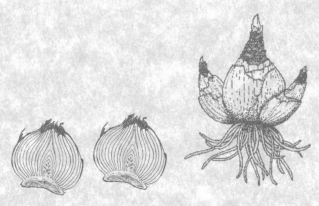

We each have to plant our own portfolio.

How would you characterize your financial investments?

Do you follow the same philosophy in your bulb portfolio? If not, why the inconsistency?

Do you think your mobility or permanence impacts your decisions botanically? fiscally?

If your answers are what I suspect, maybe we just need to invite our stockbrokers to our gardens to clarify our preferences!

*Note – when the bulb catalogs arrive each spring, I feel as if I am looking at portraits of my children or friends! Maybe landscape designers feel the same way about visiting their botanical children – watching them mature as they hoped and hoping that the owners continue their nurture.

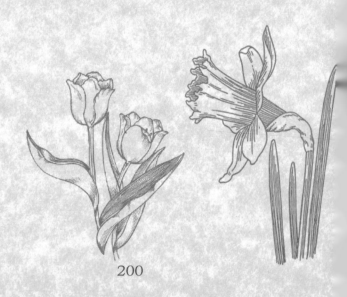

Sharing
Your Passion

Our children and now grandchildren love following my husband into his vegetable garden. Much like a secret forest, it has structures to support his Tomatoes, Sugar Snap Peas, and Cucumbers. Along the small paths, the children can find Chives, Parsley, New Zealand Spinach, and Lettuce that they are allowed to snip for salads.

Pole Beans were great attractions for our kids – the magic was climbing a ladder to pick them and then cooking them soon thereafter. If the structure supporting the beans resembled an Indian teepee, so much the better!

My herb garden yields Salad Burnet (to strip for our salad). The colorful Chards add pizzazz and little fingers get a workout picking and snipping for dinner. Seeing where food comes from and being part of the process helps us grow gardeners. Share your various passions. Even if your children and grandchildren do not adopt the same hobby, they have witnessed your commitment and delight.

Is gardening a passion you want to share with your family?

What practical results can you imagine?

What philosophical gifts do you transmit through gardening?

Through another hobby or passion?

Deadheading and Pinching Back

Gardeners know that faithfully removing the spent blooms allows plants to focus their energies on producing new blooms vs. going to seed. Near the end of their blooming seasons, some seedpods should be allowed to mature to ensure new replacements.

Likewise, gardeners can enhance the blooms of plants like Phlox, Asters, and Chrysanthemums by clipping or pinching off their early top growth. This encourages multi-branching and slows their rush to the bloom stage. Their stems become stronger in the process, better able to support the florescence ahead. Those tasks take time and timing. In our zone, the pinching-back should stop by the Fourth of July. These inglorious, disciplined actions are rewarded with healthier blooms.

How does this concept apply to our lives?

What are some of your activities that you deadhead promptly to ensure continued blooming? Fruitful production?

Does the concept of pinching back apply to our professional life? It's usually done for perennials, so we strengthen the whole plant. (e.g., Rather than having one strong, overworked leader, could pinching back his or her responsibilities enable others to blossom?)

I pinch pennies, energies expended, and outlays of emotion to ensure my future strength. These actions do require goals and discipline.

Sum and Substance

"Sum and Substance" is the name of a very large-leafed chartreuse Hosta. It is a truly noteworthy addition to your landscape. It spreads prodigiously, so you can separate out chunks in the spring to enhance other areas of your yard. My first acquaintance with 'Sum and Substance' was in the large woodland garden of a botanical friend. I coveted it mercilessly, so soon found my own. In the intervening ten years, the original has spawned three other large plants, all of which grace hillside terraces at the pond.

Have friends been a significant part in your learning and acquisition?

Have you added similar bonanzas in your professional and personal life?

Is it possible to divide these to produce even more sum and substance?

For example, my original body of work for *Family Magazine*, became the collection that formed my first *Pass It On* volume. The second volume contained some later *Family* articles, but also new chapters on leadership and life planning (lifescaping) for military families.

Have you seen overlaps in your professional and personal substance?

Lady's Slippers =
Mid-Life Effusion

We all know that Lady's Slippers are rare, protected wildflowers that do not transplant successfully. What is remarkable is that it takes a wild Lady's Slipper 10 – 17 years to mature enough to bloom – often in a colony of other Lady's Slippers whose presence has been documented over decades.

There are lessons here for ladies. How many human years would 10 – 17 year old plants be? Sounds like a mid-life effusion. And the fact that these are plants that grow in the presence of others fits the human paradigm as well.

> *When you look across your lifetime, what are the periods of greatest productivity?*
>
> *Were you part of a supportive group during those periods?*
>
> *Were you transplanted during those periods?*

Irrational Exuberance

Last year, our Chinese Dogwoods were absolutely spectacular. This year, only one branch in Mystic and nothing at the pond. A Master Gardener friend explained that they probably just wore themselves out last year and are recouping their strength this year. Ditto for the Wisteria bush with pendulous clumps overhanging the patio wall last year, and nada this spring. So, there is payback for Alan Greenspan's "irrational exuberance" even in the natural world.

My pond patio gardens have performed with irrational exuberance this spring. "Be careful what you sow," would be the pessimists' approach; but, we optimists sow with abandon, hoping that some small-to-medium percentage will produce. When our expectations are exceeded, we marvel and then have to deal with the unexpected positive results... removing excess seedlings.

A recent experience comes to mind. Our churchwomen hoped at most for a modest group for a lunch-plus-performance. Because regional newspapers, newsletters, and cable access shows featured our offering, we found ourselves with 150% of our wildest dream and up against the fire marshal's stipulated occupancy for a sit-down-lunch). Who could know?! So, for the latecomers, we could offer the performance only. They were the seedlings that had to be transplanted.

Have you had similar seasons in which the pendulum has swung from one end of the spectrum to the other?

In your personal life, how do you manage the swings?

How Do the Birds Know?

   We have a variety of bushes at the pond that have berries
in late June, and the birds know it – the Cedar Waxwings, the
Catbirds, the King Birds, and even the Sparrows. The great
attraction is the Shadblow, but also the Low-bush Blueberries.
I would love some of those little wild blueberries, but the birds
are focused on when they are ready and I am not.

*What experiences have you had with those hungrier
than you beating you to the "berries?"*

*What philosophy have you developed around this issue?
What tactics?   My resident Muskrat remembers the
fiddleheads of my Ferns. I love the Ferns too much to
compromise their productivity by eating them. No such
conscience or philosophy for the Muskrat, so I have
erected low dark green fencing around the young ferns
to deter him and put out a few mothballs.*

*When the wild Violets are in bloom, I do use some for
green salads with mushrooms – pretty and tasty.*

*What wonderful national or state parks and beaches do
we have that we fail to use for their modest fees?*

*What town or city greenways exist to be
traversed at no cost?*

*What is ripe for the picking,
botanically and otherwise?*

Moveable Feasts

Portable pots are the veritable "moveable feast." Not only can you position them where you have no in-ground possibilities, but you can aggregate them for weather and aesthetic purposes. I have some pots of red Begonias that can be plopped into an urn on our back porch for festive occasions (everyone uses our back door in Mystic); but, on a daily basis, they thrive best in a partially sunny spot at the edge of the patio. At the pond, my husband has showy pots of burgundy Elephant Ears. He can move them around for "show," but can also move them into our Mystic garage windows to over-winter.

Do we have portable achievements that can flourish wherever we go? As more people "snowbird" or move into congregate living, portable plants and projects help us carry favorites with us.

Our local garden clubs use huge "portable" pots filled with exquisite plantings to identify the houses and gardens on tour. The homeowners then are the recipients of these glorious mementos, often proudly displayed for the rest of the season.

On a personal level, a gift of a plant that can go into my garden can bring fond memories many years later. Two special friends gave me pots of Stargazer Lilies thirteen years ago as I recuperated from breast cancer. Their annual explosion reminds me of my friends' touching expression in the language of flowers.

How can we adapt this concept to our personal and professional lives?

Flower Arranging

Our church is blessed weekly with the beautiful gifts of a cadre of volunteer flower arrangers. Usually, there is a single arrangement, so the discipline of mirror-image arrangements is not required and the artist is free to express her whimsy with purchased and local garden materials. We list the arranger in the bulletin, believing that her contribution is the same as a soloist in any other domain, and that her artistry is a form of worship.

My mother had the gift of botanical arrangements, cultivated by her years as a member of various garden clubs and her lifestyle requirement for frequent entertaining on a shoestring. As a mobile Army wife, she learned to plant annuals that would provide her with showy candidates for her vases, mostly Zinnias and Dahlias. She was also a keen collector of plant materials in open fields and golf course margins! Her delight came from putting beautiful, and sometimes unlikely, partners together... a metaphor for my dad's work with NATO for about twelve years of his career – putting together remarkable, but often unlikely partners in diplomatic missions.

Have you benefited from formal training in flower arranging?

How has that impacted what you select for your garden?

Do you join me in awe of others' arrangements?

Are you an "occasional" arranger like me? Do events trigger your botanical designs?

On occasion, I have benefited from Ikebana training in Hawaii, coordinated the arrangements for an art auction using local flora in St. Marys, Georgia, and did the flowers for my mother's memorial service. I knew she would be pleased.

Quasi-Harbingers

On the first day of March, after howling winds have made me determined to remove some towering evergreens at the front corner of our Mystic property lest they crash through our bedroom ceiling, the ice and snow have almost receded (for now). When what to my wondering eyes should appear, but a solitary fat Robin, enjoying the now-black berries left on the lawn from the cut Hawthorn branches that we had piled up after heavy snows broke off a major trunk on our tree. When the dog and I retrieved the newspaper this morning, I had noticed that a lot of black berries remained on the lawn. I was not the only observer.

This lone fat Robin is not the first of his clan to visit the yard this winter. This would, perhaps, be about the appropriate time to begin to see flocks migrating and cleaning out any residual berries on their trip north. But, they were here a month ago – part of the patterns of weather change and feeder plenitude that have encouraged species to remain in areas that used to be off limits in years past. So, my lone fat Robin is no longer a true harbinger of spring. He symbolizes the radically changing climate swings and our human intrusion upon the natural order of things. So, s/he is less a harbinger than a reminder or a warning. Things are out of whack…

What have you noticed in your garden that parallels this phenomenon?

What have you noticed in human interaction patterns that indicate a change in climate (be that environmental or cultural)?

To what degree have you resisted or joined the climate change(s)?

Remember the Trojan Horse and "don't shoot the messenger" themes? How do they apply in your life?

Reflections = V³

Monet or "Mirror, mirror on the wall" reflections can amplify and transfigure our vistas, visions, and values. Somehow, the mundane cottages at our pond take on a shimmering transformation as the sun reaches them an hour before sunset. The details of reality are transmogrified into a rippled marine version of themselves – an acute reminder of the boundary between the perceived reality and the transformational. A slight breeze will give that reflection a shimmering new being, accompanied by a Kingbird's song. Impressionism on the pond…

> *The shoreline defines the separation of the two. Are our experiences in life as clearly defined?*
>
> *How do we classify our memories? Reality? Monet-esque?*
>
> *How do we select the content of our memories?*
>
> *How is this a good thing? Bad thing?*
>
> *How does sighting the Great Blue Heron on the dike across the pond help to tie the actual and the metaphorical together?**

*Hint: you remember, that the Great Blue Heron is the hero/ heroine of my book on human behaviors, *Birds of a Feather: Lessons from the Sea*. For me the underlying Jungian stories are always with us and transporting us to new dimensions.

Roots

Your roots predict your future. A plant with a taproot, such as a Globe Thistle, may spend its initial energy on its underground foundation system before demonstrating above-ground production. If it is well suited to its environment, it will be a sturdy, reliable perennial, as long as you do not attempt to move it or divide it. If transplanting is absolutely necessary, try to get as much of the root system as possible and give it lots of TLC (tender loving care).

Other plants have shallower, more horizontal roots. They do not need as deep watering as those with taproots and tend to sprout foliage quickly. Some will be annuals and others biennials (that have their showier second year and then die). Many perennials develop a woody central stem system from which both roots and new shoots appear.

People mimic these growth patterns.

Do you find that it takes you quite a while to feel comfortable in a new setting?

Do you need stability to be productive?

Do you thrive quickly wherever you are transplanted?

Do your interest and productivity wane after two years?

Do you spread your sphere of influence by mentoring or by casting your ideas far and wide to take root in favorable soils?

It's Sunset —
Do You Know Where
Your Pelican Is?

Within moments before and after sunset at Sanibel Island, Florida, strings of Pelicans are headed to their evening roost, down near the lighthouse end of the island, I suspect. Their lines over the water, arching and swooping low for the "surface effect," have their counterpoint in the silhouettes over land routes. It is almost as if their mother is ringing the family dinner bell, which all children have learned to ignore at their peril.

We have human compulsions that mimic this powerful drive, and many have garden components. For example, on this mid-February day, my husband is off looking for vegetable seeds. We have already had the deluge of seed and plant catalogs in the mail, but he is looking for the tangible packets that he can plant soon in his makeshift greenhouse to get a head start on his garden. (The rule of thumb in this region is no Tomatoes in the ground until after Memorial Day.) He will buy six-packs of some vegetables later from our nurseries.

What in our daily lives has such an unquestionable draw? If you have a pet, you know that dinner time is like clockwork.

What in our annual schedule has a similarly conditioned call?

Should we add some new ones?

P.S. I think the call to Sanibel Island fits this category for us – the relaxed rhythms, the isolation from social connections and responsibilities, the warmth, and the sheer delight in the environment – all draw us back twice a year. We carefully protect the time so that the mundane does not tarnish its allure. And we watch for the Pelicans.

212

Hope Springs Eternal

With snow still on the ground on this mid-January afternoon, I spotted our deciduous Star Magnolia from the sunroom. It is only several years old in our yard, but is about seven feet tall. There it sits leafless with apparently dormant limbs; and yet, the silver furry pods that will become the harbinger blossoms have arrived... silent reminders of the flowering to come.

The pods are metaphors for all of our embryonic ideas that burst into bloom when conditions are right.

What seemingly serendipitous happenings come to mind? To my mind today – a fund-raising project for our Women's Network that simply awaited our recognition of its tie with our goal of community outreach – a dinner theater production featuring one of our members as Louisa May Alcott.

Who are your pod-producers? Nourish and cherish them.

Give a Star Magnolia as a wedding, new house, or major achievement gift. Its very early and very showy production of exquisite blossoms is an annual reminder of the celebration. (There is a little cleanup required, but isn't that true of most great celebrations?)

Some call this species of Magnolia the *Star of Bethlehem*.

Life's Kindling

Craig Wilson, a beloved columnist with *USA Today*, wrote a column in January 2010, about gathering kindling as he walked his dog – in a nice Northern Virginia neighborhood. He struck a cord (pun on his love of well-stacked wood) with those of us who cannot throw away the gifts we find in our own yards. As former Girl and Boy Scouts, we recognize the value of those slim limbs. They will be the key to a successful start – whether our fire is to be outside or inside. My husband and I have as many "leaf barrels" filled with kindling sitting the basement as we have in operation for leaf removal in the fall. Over-kill of kindling! Also, pine cones. But, as Craig Wilson pointed out, it is free – and it removes "debris" from our yard.

Having kindling drying in the basement is like having cans of food in the pantry. It is a protection against shortage. Maybe it is our Depression–era legacy from parents who were parsimonious to survive. Maybe it is the American frontier ethic. But, for those of us who continue to live close to the land, whether we are living in the city, suburbia, or beyond, salvaging useful material is a classless compunction.

What is the kindling equivalent in your garden?

Do you have size requirements so as to avoid O'Henry's "string too short to tie?"

What is the kindling to your metaphorical fire?

Is your fire emotional? intellectual? aesthetic? spiritual?

*All of these little musings are like kindling!

214

What is so Rare...?

"What is so rare as" 45° in mid-January in New England? (Not the same winter described elsewhere in these pages!!) When the reprieve falls on a weekend, people emerge blinking in the bright sunlight (especially bright if snow is still on the ground), looking as if they have been hibernating. Certainly, the fresh air fills lungs long used to dry heating systems.

Yes, I know, the rarity is usually a day in June, and we exult in its glorious offerings as well – especially if there is a garden club tour that day!

Does a rare day bring a special sense of delight simply because of its being unusual?

Do you follow the annual and to-date records of temperature and precipitation provided in our daily newspapers? Benchmarks are used in gardening and in business to determine the baseline so that we can measure growth and exceptions. Do you use benchmarks and baselines in your professional life? personal life?

When I worked in the military family support service field, I often found it difficult to help support providers understand how truly remarkable they were. Only by sending them to national trainings and showing them the national service data could I help them measure their delivery of quantity and quality – they were "rare days in June." How do you provide that comparative measure for yourself and others?

*There is a tendency to believe that exceptional work occurs somewhere else – not "here in River City." I think it is important to celebrate the accomplishments of folks in our own environment and to see them as a prototype for provisions elsewhere.

215

Ah and Awe

"Ah" is delighted surprise when we discover something pleasant and perhaps unanticipated in the garden. "Awe" is wonder at something's beauty, ingenuity, or magnitude.

"You must come look at the sunset!" came my mother's imperative knock at the bathroom door, shortly after I had settled in to soak after a long trip to Tucson. "Now! It changes so quickly!" So, wrapped in a towel and less than amused, I found myself facing an absolutely spectacular display. At ninety-plus, she had made a ritual of watching the sun go down each night from her living room balcony and she knew that this one was a "ten" even for Tucson.*

Both experiences tend to be short-lived, but "awe" tends to linger in our memories. What have your "ah" experiences been? your "awe" experiences?

When major renovations have been done and the artistry of the landscaping choices is clear, I find myself in "awe" of the vision and the implementation of the plan. Have you had major renovations in your life that required significant investment to reach your envisioned goal?

*Seven years later, the night before I left Tucson "for good," having completed her memorial service and sent all of her precious belongings to our extended family households, I sat on her balcony and watched Awe Number Two. Quite intriguingly, a knock came at the door, and a friend of hers who had missed the gathering of the fold at dinner, came to watch it with me. It met some of her needs, as well as mine. Mom was saying, "God Be With You – Good Bye."

216

Gratitude
is an Attitude

Gardening requires courage and conviction that most of our trials and treasures will come to fruition. Each day when we survey our horticultural efforts and results, we can find something that is unusual, beautiful, or amazing. The opportunity to experience gratitude is a daily occurrence.

For example, in the last few days in our pond gardens, I have found unusual striated ball-like mushrooms pushing up through the earth, reddy-brown relatives of the usually white Indian Pipes near my Low-Bush Blueberries. (It turns out that they are Red Pinesap, a rare treat.) Mid-August with little rain has meant hours standing with a hose (from a pump in the pond) and, obviously, the time to reflect and ponder on my surroundings.

Could you approach the rest of life with the same curiosity, wonder, and gratitude?

Could a pervasive attitude of gratitude ameliorate health issues and become a self-fulfilling cure?

Could a sense of awe and wonder infuse relationships with a new dimension?

Certainly we have the power to change our own perspective and, perhaps, it may be contagious. There is no "gratitude pill" – we have to create our own ways to seize the daily opportunities – *carpe diem!* A sign at a Sanibel Island house says, *Seas the Day.* We could further the pun with *Sees the Day.*

Late Bloomers

In my garden each year there are some late bloomers – some that I know historically will be late in the season, plus a few surprises. The Monkshood, low purple Asters, perennial Ageratum, and Bugbane are givens. The unknowns are some spectacular first year Black-eyed Susans, hardy Begonias, and Dahlias. Because so many of my usual blooms are waning, these few are especially treasured.

In places where women are prevalent, like churches, small businesses, and women's business and professional networks, there is a plethora of late bloomers. Generationally, many of us now in our seventh decade and beyond faced a lifestyle where we focused on nurturing our family in our 20's and 30's. Personal growth often came later. We are now seeing the results of multiple careers and cumulative growth.

What late bloomers do you have in your garden?

Whom do you know who are late bloomers?

Who are your first season Black-eyed Susans (blooming early)? Because they are biennials at best, how do we maximize their offering?

Are there occupational fields where late bloomers are common? early bloomers?

The traditional late bloomers often have a protracted late season. They have prepared for their flowering through their long growth period. More fragile in many ways are those whose early blooms (before maturing into their second stronger year) stress the plant too heavily. Early bloomers may be spectacular, but burn out and do not return to the workplace.

218

The Anniversary Japanese Maple

For our 25th wedding anniversary, my husband and I bought a Japanese Maple. I had seen some in early fall in the Washington, DC, area as I drove to visit my parents at Walter Reed Hospital. The sunlight streaming through their leaves made them glow. A similar species at our county library was a vibrant Pomegranate red. The sun seemed to reside in the tree.

Because we were unsure how long we would be in our Arlington house (Navy orders were imminent), we kept it in its original container in the ground. The result was almost a Bonsai. Five years later, with two sets of orders in between, we moved for good back to Mystic. So, to celebrate our 30th anniversary, we planted it above the patio wall at the pond, where we would see it in all seasons.

Before long, the spectacular graft died, but the sturdy host shot up branches. This mimicked my husband's Navy retirement and new-found public office commitments and my third or fourth career – who's counting?

What does this metaphor mean to you and your career(s)? Remember that a career is really one's life's work (paid or unpaid).

When in your relationships have you reverted to original stock?

In challenging economic times, how does this apply?

Multi-tasking

Gardening brings multiple benefits. Beyond the obvious, the delight in beauty, it keeps us fit and inspires our musings. While many folks today think that multi-tasking involves a variety of electronic devices, those of us who toil in our yards know that the physical exertion of planting, raking, pruning, and dead-heading frees up our alpha waves for significant thought. The beta waves are the doing-right-now short-term activity. The alpha waves permit subconscious explorations. I often keep a pad of paper and pen close at hand so that I can jot down concepts that waft by.

Studies of electronic multi-tasking generally show that the short attention (beta waves) to each execution produces mediocre performance in all domains. Maybe that is enough for some tasks; however, for creative endeavors, the alpha waves are requisite.

There are some basic tasks like canning, gardening, vacuuming, house painting, etc. that do not involve us intellectually all of the time and, therefore, enable the alpha wave activity. Which activities enable this for you?

Do you find that time has no meaning for you in your garden? Is that because your mind is elsewhere?

How can you maximize the visionary aspect of gardening and other similar activities? Have you tried tasking your subconscious with a problem to solve or a creative product to explore?

Solitude would be an important ingredient in this process.

Five Miles Per Hour

Yes, you read that correctly – five miles per hour! That is the speed limit on Long Pond. Speed signs provided by the Town of Ledyard often bring a chuckle from kayakers and canoeists, but a snarl (or worse) from bass boaters. Even though the public boat launch at the head of the pond, one mile away, is very clear about the speed limit, some boaters have trouble remembering by the time they get to us.

The speed limit is set by the town to protect docks, piers, and stone walls. Long Pond is long and narrow, so wake impacts areas where Wood Ducks, Swans, Mallards, and Otters nest. And yes, speed impacts the very fish that bring the fishermen. You would think that broad self-interest would prevail.

What domains does this remind you of?

How would lower speeds in other areas of our lives be beneficial?

How does consideration of both nature and the man-made environment improve our condition?

Some Crave Crowds

In order to be productive, some plants crave crowds or, at least, can tolerate them. Black-eyed Susans, Coneflowers, perennial Ageratum, Phlox, and Evening Primroses come to mind. Others really must be divided periodically in order to blossom, such as Iris and Daffodils.

People fall into the same categories, needing the stimulus of people around them or requiring quiet, uninterrupted periods in order to be fruitful. Which are you?

Do you seek out others to energize you and find that your best ideas come when triggered by others?

Do you absolutely need a solitary environment for blocks of time to do your best work?

Or, are you a hybrid, relishing others' interaction in the beginning of a project, but wanting time removed from "the madding crowd" to sort and solidify your course of action?

The fourth style is the flip of the hybrid above – desiring solitary thought first and then joining a group to coalesce and expedite your plan.

Just as a good gardener needs to understand his or her plants for the ideal landscape, you need to understand your requirements for your ideal lifescape. Do no less for yourself than you would do for your garden. In your workplace, do no less for those with whom you work.

Fiddleheads –
Truth Unfolding

The Fern's fiddlehead fills me with awe. When it first shows as a furry velvet knob close to the earth, it does not advertise its presence or its potential. Ever so slowly it emerges as a tightly wound fist, clasping its secrets lest they become known before their time. Each day brings a combination of height and a slight unwinding. Timed exposures show a stately and yet sinuous choreography of the utmost restraint and beauty. When it reaches its full height, it slowly unwraps its incredibly compacted leaf – a crenellated marvel.

Whenever hungry creatures rob me of a fiddlehead (Muskrats come to mind), I feel somehow violated. Cut off before its prime, before it could become – its stalk left as a bare nub – it fills me with sadness. This unconscious reaction must be wound up in a deep emotional well whose meaning I cannot quite decipher. For me the unfolding fiddlehead signifies the emergence of Nature's Truth.

What encounters have you had in your garden that seem more profound than the superficial experience?

If you lose someone at a young age, do you wonder what she or he might have become?

How about the loss of a project or a relationship in its infancy?

When do you sit still long enough to ponder the potential?

Do you value the slow-to-unfold and mature?

Portable Pots

For those with limited sunny spots and those wanting to grow plants that cannot over-winter outside, pots are ideal. Also, when soil is bad or non-existent, a pot offers a rich microcosm in which to grow. Our lives can mimic this phenomenon. When our pace is too hectic or our environment devoid of nourishment, spending time in an enriched microcosm can help us blossom, be fruitful, or at least winter-over.

How can we make our best-self portable? Two different years, three years apart, I treated myself to the Wesleyan Writers Workshop at Wesleyan University in Middletown, Connecticut. This weeklong intensive course enabled writers to submit samples of their work to mentors who would be teaching during the week and who would provide a one-on-one critique of their work. The first year, I had moved back to Arlington, Virginia, from Kings Bay Georgia, the week before the course, so I was truly in transition. The second time, I had started a new journalism-intensive job in Connecticut and was able to use my civil service training funds to enhance skills and perspectives specific to my new situation. Both times the hothouse kind of existence allowed me to focus just on growing my writing skills.

How can you make your best-self portable?

Can technology help?

Does geography play a role?

What feeds your productivity?

Conversely, what stymies your growth?

Don't Tread on Fragile Ground

Many of us have experienced extremely wet springs lately. It almost breaks my heart to see water standing in areas of my perennial garden. I wonder if my vibrant low orange Lilies will survive their watery-feet-and-freeze activity. Each year I vow to build up those low spots (and I do), but our property drains a large cul-de-sac community just a little higher up on our granite-based hill. Gravity is against us! So is the clay layer about 6 – 8 inches below the surface. No amount of coffee grounds mixed into the soil is going to alleviate that problem. Prayer time!

The least I can do is not step in the garden areas that have been subjected to this seasonal flooding. I can exercise all sorts of muscles to weed, snip, and even plant without setting my compacting feet on tender beds.

Gardens we can see. People are harder, especially when they have been flooded by stress, sorrow, or sadness. How can we be equally careful of their fragile state and yet provide some assistance that does not further compact their challenges?

Knowing the boundaries is important for garden beds and people.

Recognizing that fragility can be a temporary condition is helpful.

Realizing that we can build physical and emotional muscles as we stretch ourselves can be a lesson in resilience.

Give a Garden Party

Just as homeowners know that committing to a party or house tour gets them doing all of the renovations they have had on their wish list, a call from your local non-profit agency or garden club will set you a-twitter. For those who need deadlines to accomplish their dreams, this is an agony/ecstasy dichotomy come true. Motivation is personal and powerful.

I give an annual pizza party in our Mystic garden for current Smith College students and 17 local high school book award winners. This is low-key recruitment and retention with a dose of parents and alumnae. Because so many of our alumnae are remarkable gardeners, my husband and I always go the extra mile in late August to trim the walkways and driveway, cut the errant growth on bushes, deadhead and weed the gardens, and then put our vast collection of chairs and tables out under the Redbud tree. (The garden furniture is mostly the result of culling give-aways at our town's recycling center!).

We delight in sharing our gardening passion with these young students. Research has shown that when adult role models share their commitment to a hobby, their passion is contagious – not necessarily for their specific focus, but for the generic philosophy.

Do you accomplish more with deadlines looming?

Does external observation of your work heighten your resolve?

Do you see opportunity in challenges, or just risk?

226

Sheds

In our neck of the Southeastern Connecticut "woods," lots of folks have sheds. Some are former garages that are now too small for today's cars. Others never had a cement floor. They were simply built raised up off of a dirt or gravel base (so may have problems with rot). Ours at the pond had to be replaced for this reason, so we copied the footprint exactly, including the space that was the old privy – now my gardening tool shed. The bigger portion has been designed to hold a variety of kayaks, paddles, life jackets, and tools for maintaining the property. These sheds have a magical quality, much like that of children's play houses. They stand alone and are not regularly inhabited. Our grandchildren would love to spend the night in the boat shed when they are just a bit older.

Anne Morrow Lindbergh had a shed (both at Captiva Island, Florida where her *Gifts from the Sea* was inspired, and at the Lindbergh estate to which she returned and where she actually wrote the book – secluded from family and the world).

My "rooms of my own" have ranged from a tiny guest bedroom in our first house (a circa 1860 barn in Quaker Hill, CT), to a balcony overlooking our patio in Vallejo, CA (a 1920's doll house), to a big hall closet with sliding doors in Navy housing in Charleston, SC. Another really important "shed" was the former maid's room in the basement of our 1930's Arlington, VA house. It served as my office for a decade's worth of magazine articles for military families.

Where do you find your own equivalent of a shed?

Why is it so important to your gardening?

To your creativity?

Strange Bedfellows

What's in a name? Well, if you're talking about plant families, there has been the expectation that the family members will bear an obvious resemblance to each other. However, the use of DNA to categorize family members under the revolutionary system APG III (Angiosperm Phylogeny Group) has moved Indian Pipes to the same family as Azaleas and Blueberries – Ericaceae. It is like learning that you are adopted! Or, that your astrological sign has been off kilter for two thousand years!

So now, Indian Pipes have joined the Heathers and Azaleas. While I have always been intrigued by the quiet emergence of the Indian Pipes from matted leaves at the pond, and astonished by a new red-stemmed variety on the bank filled with Low-Bush Blueberries this past year, I have seen them as more of a Fungus or Mushroom kind of growth. It just goes to show that visual appearance may mask the true nature of an individual.

What relationship surprises have you experienced – botanically?

What relationship surprises have you experienced in the human world?

When have you been surprised by visual appearances?

I Saved a Swallowtail Butterfly Today

There he was – a yellow and black pair of wings, folded and caught struggling in a spider's web. Periodically struggling to extricate himself, he must not have been there long. After batting the web loose, I dropped him and the residual web on the ground nearby. Stunned, he did not move for a little while. I went back to my watering. When I next turned around, he was slowly making his way up a Firetail plant, soon resting flat out on the top leaf.

Some time later, he came fluttering around me, as if to say, "Thank you!" His life is so short, he deserves to enjoy every minute of it.

When has someone helped to extricate you from a web?

When have you done likewise?

Was a heartfelt "Thank you!" part of the deal(s)?

Were there any strings attached?

Did the process of saving/being saved connect you with the other?

Was there a sense of being a part of the larger system of Nature?

Was there a sense of rational intervention in a non-rational system?

Garden Clubs

Many wonder why I am not a garden club member. Both my mother and my mother-in-law were members, and loved their affiliation and service. The latter is the rub for me. I admire the service projects planted, nourished, and supported by our regional clubs and I attend their tours with a passion, a buddy, and a camera. But, my personal and professional focus has been on military families, an all-consuming sponge of my time and energies. So, gardening has been my respite. I believe that I need to be careful in guarding some of my sources of pleasure from becoming others' avenues to consuming my time and turning "delights" into "oughts." Music and gardening are two domains that come to mind.

That said, one of my fondest memories is working at sunset one early December evening on the two cider barrels that graced the entry to the Navy Family Service Center, where I served as director. I had unloaded Bayberry, Yew, Juniper, and Winterberry branches from my car after work and was happily stabbing them into not-yet-frozen dirt. A Navy chief walked by and said, "Didn't I see you filling the window boxes in downtown Mystic this week?" I realized that my white hair and age fit the profile. "Nope, but those were a bunch of my friends who are in the garden club." I was pleased to be presumed to be part of their company.

Do you have domains that you need to protect as "delights?"

Are there groups from which you can learn without formal affiliation?

Can you assist groups without formal affiliation (e.g., by attending their fund-raising events and by offering raw materials, contacts, and word-of-mouth publicity?)

Planting Forward

A concept that is popular these days is giving forward...instead of paying back. It involves investing in something or someone that has yet to become, and is at a critical stage when nurture and support would make a quantum difference in the outcome. In our gardens, planting bulbs in the fall is one example. The iconic ad that shows young hands planting a small tree sends this message.

Just as wise investors seek out companies that are on the cusp of significance, we can search out products or causes that may improve people's lives. We are planting our finances and our faith in their ability to make a positive difference.

How can you use your skills and passions to teach young people how to garden (literally and metaphorically)?

Recognizing that it is often impossible to pay back those who made a difference in our lives, we can strive to "pass it on." What have you passed on?

What major undertakings can you get off the ground that will produce far into the future?

Peek Experiences

No – that is not a typographical error! I suspect we could have peak peek experiences… those that are both surreptitious and heart-stopping! Peak experiences are those glorious moments that we see as the epitome of our being. A recent Oscar Award winner remarked that his career had probably peaked in the winning role – my reaction was that it was probably one of many peaks that he can attain. There you have it – my optimism – but Malcolm Gladwell, in his book *The Outliers* (2008), makes it clear that those who practice and focus for an extensive amount of time (10,000 hours) on achieving skills or performing creatively, are likely to have multiple peak achievements. Longevity is helpful, too.

However, my focus here is on "peek experiences" – those in which we observe something mysterious, delightful, or known-only-to-us. I have had several recently: one was discovering a Garter Snake peering at me from the top of the barrel of leaves that I had just cleared from the early spring pond gardens. Clearly, I had picked him up in a somnolent state (unbeknownst to me!), and he had migrated to the top of the barrel to barely flick his tongue when I lifted the cover off to add more leaves. (My husband ensured that he found a new home near a low rock wall.)

The Bullfrog in the murky waters by our pond boat launch area astounded my daughter-in-law. She had heard him the night before, but could not believe his actual size when our son pointed him out to her and the grandkids. The volume that echoes down the pond is disproportionate to his actual size (he sounds like a "boom box" as he courts all of the females within a couple of miles); but he is a relatively large frog by amphibian standards. We peek to see if he is enjoying his leafy muck, but never disturb him.

We have another visitor, as yet unseen – but a peek is hoped for: a Beaver. Last summer, he and his family blocked the culvert through which we kayak to an adjacent pond. We had to pull all sorts of branches out of the way to pass through. At first, I suspected a human; but then the telltale signs of sharp teeth indicated the real suspect. Now, s/he has felled a medium-sized tree on the edge of our property – not quite sliced clean, so my husband will remove it once warm weather permits (if he is not too late). It would impede kayakers in the area. I would love to peek at the Beaver at work.

What have you longed to peek at?

What have you peaked at?
professionally?
personally?
botanically?

Are there other peaks ahead?

Ivy Wreathes
the Pines

As the officially designated "blizzard" begins to melt on the day before Christmas, our Pine trees have mounded Ivy wreaths encircling them. What a lovely view from our windows, with a touch of red Winterberries in my peripheral vision. The Birds and Squirrels also delight in these green patches that provide sources of food in an otherwise snow-covered yard.

The Ivy bed at the foot of the Pines blends with Pachysandra at both ends of its extent. Not only does this lessen the amount of grass to mow, but it provides evergreen camouflage for the endless needles, cones, and twigs that the Pines generate. Once a year, I must cut back the Ivy tendrils climbing the trees, but it is a small price to pay for this unanticipated and unintended consequence.

Do you have unintended consequences in your garden? Favorable or unfavorable?

Have you experienced unintended consequences in your life? Favorable or unfavorable?

How have you dealt with the unfavorable consequences?

The favorable?

Positive outcomes that seem serendipitous may have had their seeds in acts that you consciously or unconsciously sowed long ago. While we often say that we were "lucky," in retrospect, these fortunate occurences may be less random than they seem. Malcolm Gladwell's books, *The Tipping Point* (2000) and *Outliers* (2008), address this phenomenon and provide strategies for increasing one's positive, intended consequences.

Directed Dreaming

When you're worried and cannot sleep,
Try counting your blessings instead of sheep,
And you'll fall asleep counting your blessings.

When you have trouble sleeping or are facing troublesome days, you might want to try the strategy of directed dreaming. The concept is like putting a DVD into your brain of something that brings you pleasure to supplant the worrisome thoughts.

One favorite theme is to picture a house or a garden that you love and walk yourself through it detail by detail. An enhancement of this motif is to redesign the house or garden with no concerns about cost or effort. I like this part best!

When I had knee surgery two years ago, my husband and I had just returned from a Caribbean cruise (highly recommended as pre-surgery therapy!). When seemingly endless blocks of time lay ahead before pain medication could be administered, I mentally created a clothing line based on the exotic flowers we had recently encountered. If only I could draw in real life!

When has "reel life" comforted you?

Have your gardens played a role in that?
(e.g., could you pretend in your dream state that Martha Stewart has come to you for a feature article on gardening – what could you share?)

Could you design the tool or tool shed of your dreams?

Weary, Dirty, and Satisfied

How often have you finished a session in your garden exhausted, sweaty, dirty, and delighted by your efforts? You notice I said "efforts" and not "successes." The latter would be gratifying, but the truth is that we can only calibrate the former.

Much of life presents a parallel commitment of well-intentioned work with hard-to-measure results. Think of the efforts of social workers, ministers, and educators — absolute bedrock professions in our society. We can quantify the moisture, fertilizer (organic, of course), sunlight, and temperatures our gardens have experienced; and, to some degree, we can gauge the "return." Human endeavors are less predictable.

How do you measure satisfaction?
Success?

Is there a reliable ratio of effort to results?

What are the variables?

In philosophical and religious domains,
we encounter the same dilemma. Efforts do not
equate to nirvana. We must leave room for grace –
unearned, simply a gift.

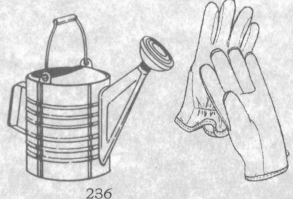

Winter of My Content

A recent front-page headline in our local newspaper was "Winter of Our Discontent." I rushed to my Bartlett's to remember that the original was indeed Shakespeare (*Richard III*). My husband remembered John O'Hara. But, it has been my winter of content; in spite of travel and shoveling woes, I have been able to hunker down and really focus on this book and designing curricula for some courses I will teach.

My garden beds have been blessedly blanketed with white insulation. Yes, some bushes are challenged with the heavy snow, but we have been able to wade through the snow, armed with garden rakes, and have been able to free them from their burdens. You can almost hear their exultation as their branches spring back. We have been forced to slow down, cancel programs that can be rescheduled in fairer weather, and just enjoy our Black Labrador romping in the snow. He knows... this is fun! My snowballs melt in his mouth and he asks for more.

Why are the changing seasons important to you?

What does each season bring as its own special offering?

What would it be like to live where little changes from one season to the next?

What would not thrive in such a climate?

What would thrive?

We lived for two years on the coast at the Georgia – Florida border. The seasonal changes were much subtler than those in the Northeast. I realized that the combination of having lived in mostly four-season climates, plus having spent significant professional time as a teacher (with the summer off to replenish) meant that I was ill-suited for a place like Aruba or Grenada where the seasons and the tide barely change. Could I eventually adapt?

Lights in the Snow

How bravely they have melted through the banks of snow –
our dear little electric pathway lights that illuminate our pond
patio and Mystic front walkway. They have been buried under
mounds of ice and snow for weeks, and yet tonight are burning
bright.

Their lights have been hiding under the proverbial bushels (of
snow), not of their own choosing. Both functional and decorative,
they now shine with reflected glory with white orbs around their
base. They raise our spirits with their new-found brilliance.
They look like little space ships ready to launch into outer space…
or, as the case may be, into our inner space.

When have you felt as if your light has been buried?

When finally free, has your glow been magnified?

*Let your light so shine before men, that they may see
your good works, and glorify your Father
which is in heaven.*

Matthew 5: 16, King James version of the Bible

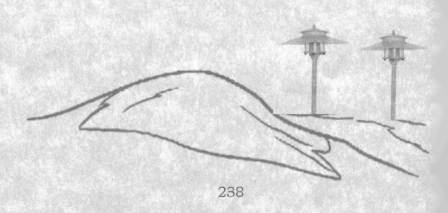

238

The Fruits
of Our Labors

Tonight by the fireplace at the pond, I cannot help but be grateful for our labors-past. We are warmed and enchanted by our fire – supplied by all of those twigs and branches collected in the yard.

Our pond room is the result of caring Mystic neighbors who helped us bleach our walls and cupboards when we first bought the house, and remove the mildew-causing cork floor tiles covered with indoor-outdoor felt carpeting. Our elbow grease with tongue oil restored the pine paneling to its glory. Terracotta ceramic tiles laid by a craftsman, who brought his family to join him for lunches, cured the source problem. His wife told me, "We loved your cabin even before you moved in!"

This spot on Long Pond, while technically ours, is the result of many labors past – those of previous Indian inhabitants, owners past, and friends and craftsmen who have given their talents to its current incarnation. They and we are all stewards of this special place.

What else do we steward?

Do we remember to recognize the contributions of others?

Who will shepherd our domains in the future?

Have we helped to prepare them?

239

Epilogue

Most of these musings have been written on scraps of paper, kept handy for the purpose. Some are excess flyers from the Community Coalition for Children... helping children thrive®. Others are leftovers from the Mystic Congregational Church requests for children's winter clothing (on mitten motif cards). The blank sides of Christmas cards too pretty to recycle, the leftover bazaar and tag sale flyers from Women's Fellowship, and my old business cards – all sit at the cabin on Long Pond, awaiting inspiration, and in my Mystic kitchen drawer, expecting memories while I am cooking.

I cannot imagine producing such a book without practicing what I preach. All drafts were printed on flyers for my now out-of-print books on military families. How nice that the books are all out helping the folks I love and the PR paper is being recycled for a book on gardening.

Remember to call Lisa!

- Bird seed
- Bread
- Eggs

Index

Ageratum, perennial *(Conoclinium collestinum)* .... *54, 59,112, 119, 126, 127, 139* *182, 189, 218, 222*

Alder, Swamp *(Ilex)* *9, 30, 68*

Apple tree 9

Armeria *(see* Sea Pink, Thrift*)* 67

Aster, New England *(Aster novae-angliae – wildflower)* *54, 162*

Aster *(both tall and short cultivars)* *17, 33, 54, 108, 202, 162*

Aucuba, Japanese Laurel 112, 113, 116, 156, 173

Azalea 13, 62, 108, 228

Baby Blue Eyes *(Veronica 'Bergen's Blue')* *54, 119, 173, 205*

Beautyberry *(Callicarpa americana)* 30, 68, 109

Bedstraw, also known as Sweet Woodruff 119, 148

Bee Balm *(Monarda)* 79, 127, 173, 179

Beech, Copper *(Fagus sylvatica)* 62

Begonia 35, 52, 176, 207, 218

Bellflower *(Campanula)* 65, 112, 143

Birch, River *(Betula nigra)* 30

Bittersweet 138, 159, 173

Black-eyed Susan *(Rudbeckia serotina)* 59, 62, 84, 115, 127, 188, 218, 222

Blazing Star *(Liatris)* – see also Gay Feathers 108

Blueberry, Low bush *(Vaccinium)* 206, 228

Blue-eyed Grass *(Sisyrinchium graminoides)* 169, 173, 198

Broom, Scotch *(Cytisus scoparius)* 12, 119, 173

Bugbane, Black *(Actaea simplex 'Brunette')* 57, 62, 65, 79, 218

Burning Bush *(Euonymus)* 16, 20, 138, 158

Caladium *(Caladium)* 82

Campion, Rose *(Lychnis coronaria)* 115

Campion, Royal Catchfly *(Silene 'Rollie's Favorite')* 67

Cardinal Flower *(Lobelia)* 65, 157

Chicory 198

Chives 24, 25, 173, 185

Chrysanthemum 17, 33, 202

Clematis 153

Coleus 33

Columbine, wild *(Aquilegia canadensis)* 54, 115, 169, 173

Coneflower *(Echinacea)* 23, 54, 59, 62, 84, 127, 189, 222

Copper Beech *(Fugus sylvatica)* 62

Coral Bells *(Heuchera)* 62

Cosmos 52, 60, 62, 67, 84

Crabapple tree *(Malus 'Radiant')* 5, 9, 68, 113

Crabgrass 161

Cuphea 61

Daffodils 128, 199, 222
Daisy, English/Ox-eye *(Chrysanthemum Leucanthemum)*.......................54
Daisy, Marguerite & painted *(Chrysantemum pyrethrum)* 57
Daisy, Montauk *(Nipponanthemum nipponicum)* 108
Daisy, Shasta (*Chrysanthemum superbum*)........................ 79, 127, 147
Daisy *(Scabiosa)*... 61
Day Lily *(Hemerocallis)* - see Lily
Dogwood, American *(Cornus florida)* 16, 20, 119
Dogwood, Chinese *(Cornus kousa chinensis)* 16, 17, 173, 205
Elephant Ears, black *(Colocasia esculenta 'Black Magic')*...........35, 64, 147, 207
Euonymus *(dark green and variegated)* 56
Evening Primrose *(Oenothera biennis)* ... 27, 20, 54, 63, 139, 158, 173, 188, 222
False Indigo, yellow *(Baptisia)* 65
False Solomon's Seal *(Smilacina racemosa)* 162, 169, 173
Fern, Cinnamon *(Osmunda cinnaomea)* 52, 54, 175, 188
Fern, fiddlehead *(this is a stage vs. a species)* 173, 175, 206, 223
Fern, Ostrich *(Matteuccia struthiopteris)* 52, 164, 175, 188
Fern, Sensitive *(Onoclea sensibilis)* 158, 173, 175
Feverfew or Sneezewort *(Tanacetum/Chrysanthemum parthenium* 115
Firethorn *(Pyracantha)*... 109
Forget-Me-Not (False) *(Brunnera macrophylla "Variegata')*
see also Siberian Bugloss 67
Forsythia 56
Fountain Grass, Purple *(Pennisetum setaceum)* 188
Foxtail Lilies *(Eremus)* 65
Funkia (also Plantain Lily) *(see Hosta)*
Gay Feathers *(Liatris)* see also Blazing Star 108
Geranium *(pelargondium)*..35, 61
Hawthorn *(Cratageus)* 5, 69, 152, 163, 209
Hawkweed *(Hieracium)* 115
Heal-All *(Prunella vulgaris)* 162
Holly, American *(Ilex opaca)* 9
Holly, Golden Berry *(Ilex crenata 'Golden Gem')*.............................9, 56
Holly *(Ilex 'Nellie Stevens')* 9, 56
Holly *(Ilex meservae 'Blue Prince')* 9, 154
Honeysuckle *(Lonicera)*.. 177
Hosta, Plantain Lily *(also called Funkia)* 18, 51, 57, 62, 116, 173
Hosta *('Sum & Substance')*.. 116, 203
Hyacinth, Grape *(Muscari)*.. 205
Hyacinth *(Hyancinthus 'orientalis')* 199
Indian Pipes *(Monotropa uniflora)* 95, 169, 173, 217, 228

Inkberry *(Ilex glabra)* 9, 30, 56, 68
Iris, Siberian *('sibirica')* 54, 79, 119, 126, 127, 222
Ixora 86
Jasmine *(Jasminium 'Moonbeam')* 57
Juniper *(Juniperis)* 230
Lady's Mantle *(Alchemilla)* 112, 116, 164
Lady's Slipper *(Cypripedium)* 95, 173, 174, 204
Lavender *(Lavandula)* 178, 188
Liatris *(see Blazing Star & Gay Feathers)*
Lily of the Valley *(Convallaria majalis)* 15, 95, 173, 178
Lily of the Valley, Wild *(Maianthemum canadense)* 173
Lily, Stargazer *(Lilium 'Stargazer')* 108, 178, 207
Lily, Surprise *(Colchicum cilicicum)* 185
Lily, Tiger *(Lilium lancifolium trigrinum)* 54, 87, 173
Lion's Foot, Wild Lettuce *(Lactuca spp.)* 95, 173
Loosestrife *(Lysimachia)* 54
Lungwort *(Pulmonaria)* 162
Magnolia, Star *(Magnolia stellata 'Star of Bethlehem')* 13, 113, 213
Maltese Cross *(Lychnis chalcedonica)* 62
Maple, Japanese *(Acer ornatum Dissectum Atropurpureum)* 27, 62, 173, 219
Maple, Swamp *(Acer rubrum)* 16, 20
Money Plant *(Lunaria)* 107
Monkshood *(Aconitum)* 17, 27, 159, 218
Moss, Hair-cap *(Polytrichum commune)* 5, 95, 173, 177, 179
Mountain Ash *(Sorbus)* 17
Mountain Laurel *(Kalmia latifolia)* 13, 173, 177
Myrtle, purple & white (aka Periwinkle) *(Vinca minor)* 13, 90, 173
Nine Bark tree/bush *(Physocarpus opulifolius 'Monlo')* 62
Oxalis, pink 198
Pachysandra 13, 90, 116-17, 158, 234
Pearly Everlasting *(Saxifrage, Anaphalis margaritacea)* 173
Peony *(Paeonia)* 82, 177
Periwinkle (See Myrtle*)*
Phlox, Creeping *(Phlox subulata)* 119
Phlox (low lavender or blue) *(Phlox divaricata)* 169, 173, 205
Phlox, tall *(Phlox paniculata)* 54, 79, 126, 202, 222
Pine, Austrian *(Pinus nigra)* 150
Pine, White *(Pinus parviflora)* 50, 75, 113, 138, 234

Pipsissewa, Spotted Wintergreen, Prince's Pine
(Chimaphila maculata/umbellata) 5, 173
Poppies *(Papaver orientale)* 173, 205
Pyracantha 109
Purpletop Vervain *(Verbena bonariensis)* 115
Queen Anne's Lace *(Daucus carota)* 198
Redbud *(Cercis canadensis)* 5, 52, 62, 64, 67, 113, 156, 188
Red-Hot Poker *(Kniphofia)* 65
Red Pinesap *(Hypopitys monotropa)* 217
Rose Campion, soft gray leaves *(Lychnis coronaria)* 115
Rose of Sharon *(Hibiscus syriacus)* 143-44
Royal Catchfly *(Silene)* 67
Sage *(Salvia officionalis)* 184
Salad Burnet *(Sanguisorba minor)* 116, 185, 201
Scilla *(Scilla sibirica)* 82, 171
Sea Pink, Thrift *(Armeria maritime)* 67
Shadblow, Shadbush, Saskatoon Serviceberry *(Amelanchier alnifolia)* 206
Shasta Daisy *(Chrysanthemum leucanthemum)* 79, 127, 147
Sheep Sorrel *(Rumehastatulus)* 142, 173
Siberian Bugloss *(Brunnera macrophylla 'Variegata')*
see also Forget-Me-Not - 67
Smoke Bush, purple *(Cotinus coggygria 'Royal Purple')* 5, 62, 113
Sneezewort *(Achilleaptarmica)* see also Feverfew 115
Solomon's Seal (False) *(Smilacina racemosa)* 228
Sorrel, Sheep, also known as Wild Dock *(Rumex hastatulus)* 142, 173
Sparkleberry *(Ilex serrata x verticillata 'Sparkleberry')* 9, 30, 114
Spiderwort *(Tradescanthia)* 54, 173
Spotted Wintergreen, Pipsissewa *(Chimaphila maculata)* 5, 173
Spurge, burgundy *(Euphorbia amygdaloides 'Purpurea')* 63
Sweet Woodruff, also called Bedstraw *(Galium odoratum)* 119, 148, 173
Tansy *(Tanacetum vulgare)* 196
Thistle, Globe *(Echinops)* 79, 84, 211
Touch-Me-Not *(Impatiens capensis)* 143-44, 173
Trailing Arbutus *(Epigaea repens)* 95, 173
Trout Lily *(Erythronium 'Pagodo')* 140
Tulip, little hybrids *(e.g. 'Tinka')* 110, 169, 199
Tulip, 'Monsella' 199
Tulip, 'Parrot' 199
Tulip, 'Rembrandt' 199
Winterberry *(Ilex verticillata)* 5, 9, 27, 30, 68, 114, 230
Wisteria 173, 205
Witch Hazel *(Hamamelis 'Arnold's Promise')* 13, 170
Yellow Rocket *(Barbarea vulgaris arcuata)* 198

Bibliography

Always, Sara, *Soil Mates: Companion Planting for Your Vegetable Garden*, Quirk Books (Phila., 2010).

Embertson, Jane, *Pods: Wildflowers and Weeds in Their Final Beauty,* Charles Scribner's Sons (NY, 1979).

Gladwell, Malcolm, *Outliers: The Story of Success,* Little, Brown and Co. (NY, 2008).

Gladwell, Malcolm, *The Tipping Point: How Little Things Can Make a Big Difference,* Little, Brown and Co. (NY, 2000).

Klimas, Dr. John E., Jr., *Wildflowers of Connecticut*, published for the Audubon Society, State of CT (Walker & Co, NY, 1968).

O'Beirne, Kathleen P., *Birds of a Feather: Lessons from the Sea*, Lifescape Enterprises (Mystic, CT, 2006).

*Other books are referenced in the text and may be out of print.

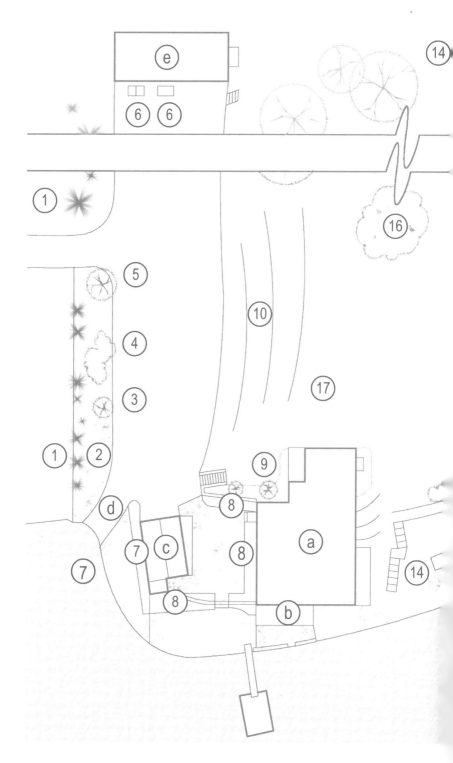

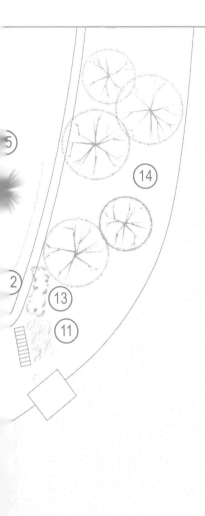

Long Pond

1 Evergreens

2 Pachysandra

3 Redbud

4 Aucuba

5 Chinese Dogwood

6 Raised Beds

7 Shed Bank Bed

8 Patio Beds

9 Wisteria

10 Hostas

11 Grasses

12 Sweet Woodruff

13 Wild Blueberries

14 Woodlands

15 Lady's Slippers

16 Glacial Rocks

17 Moss

a house

b porch

c shed

d boat launch

e rental

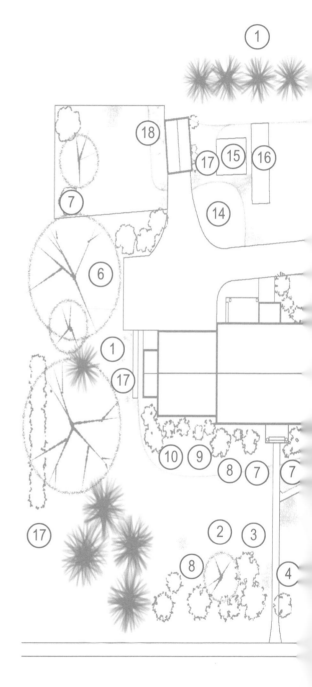

Mystic Gardens

1 Pines

2 Crabapples

3 Mountain Laurels

4 Hawthorn Tree

5 Swamp Alder

6 Maples

7 Aucubas

8 Inkberries

9 Hollies

10 Beautyberry

11 Star Magnolia

12 Redbud

13 Dogwoods

14 Oval Garden

15 Vegetable Garden

16 Main Garden

17 Winterberries

18 Ground Cover

Gardens I Have Known and Loved

    Our experience with gardens shapes us. As a little girl in Arlington, Virginia, I was given a small backyard plot of my own. My family lived next door to the only ravine park in the county, so I spent glorious hours roaming its Laurel- and Rhododendron-covered banks and investigating the swampy area where Skunk Cabbage grew and slithering creatures congregated. Years later, as an undergraduate at Smith College, I loved the botanical gardens and the conservatory. As a member of the Alumnae Association Board and a frequent attendee at reunions, I have found the college gardens a reference for my own gardens... lifetime learning at its best.

    The bulk of my adult gardening has taken place in Southeastern Connecticut and Arlington (during my husband's tours at the Pentagon). My first Connecticut garden was enclosed by the stone walls around a Civil War barn. My predecessor had already stocked it with wonderful perennials. But, the move into our Mystic house occasioned planting a green screen on two sides of our very public corner, plus vegetable and flower gardens. Our property at Long Pond, in Ledyard, is glacial residue – tough soil, but delightful vistas.

    Our Mystic corner propelled me into historic district and environmental activism as our community fought an intrusive connector from I-95. As president of T.R.E.E.S. (To Reassess Ecology-Environment-Safety), I was disappointed that we lost the highway battle, but we successfully spear-headed the designation of an Historic District and the acquisition of the Pequot Woods by the Town of Groton – 400 acres of glacial ravine and brook that ensures a greenbelt legacy.

    Additional locations where my husband and I have lived and gardened include Vallejo, CA, Honolulu, HI, Charleston, SC, and Kings Bay, GA. Other influences include frequent travels to my parents' retirement home in Tucson, AZ, and our forays into the Caribbean. The Caribbean gardens, plus my own, have propelled me into photography as a way to really look at the micro-beauty around me. The resulting botanical note cards are a joy to share. So, these are my "green credentials."

Kathleen Parker O'Beirne

What are the ingredients for thinking and writing about leadership?

Smith College (B.A.) and Wesleyan University (M.A.L.S.)

Navy wife of a submariner and mother of two cherished children

Girl Scout and Scout leader for 7 troop years

Associate Editor, *Family Magazine* for 12 years

Public Affairs Officer and Program Manager (for spouse employment and volunteer management), Department of Defense Office of Family Policy and Support and Public Affairs Officer, Naval Underwater Systems Center, New London, CT

Director, Navy Family Service Center, Naval Submarine Base, New London, CT

Teacher/Instructor: junior high through university post-graduate levels (including the National Defense University)

Boards of Directors: USO World Board, Alumnae Association of Smith College, Southeastern CT Women's Network, Military Child Education Coalition & Community Coalition for Children (SE CT)

Leadership Awards: Navy Wife of the Year, Outstanding Woman of the Year (both Camden County, GA BPW and S.E.CT Women's Network), Department of the Navy Meritorious Civilian Service Award, Athena Award, United Church of Christ CT "Recognized Woman," and Moderator, Mystic Congregational Church

Re-order Information

__ __   copies of **Mobile Student Passport** ($6.00)
ISBN 978-1-879979-06-3

__ __   copies of **Life Is a Beach: Musings from the Sea** ($14.95)
ISBN 978-1-879979-09-8

__ __   copies of **Birds of a Feather: Lessons from the Sea** ($19.95)
ISBN 978-1-879979-02-0

__ __   copies of **Birds of a Feather: Behavior Patterns Matrix** ($5.00)
ISBN 978-1-879979-03-9

__ __   copies of **Birds of a Feather: Educator's Guide** ($5.00)
ISBN 978-1-879979-11-X

__ __   copies of **Birds of a Feather: Parent's Guide** ($5.00)
ISBN 978-1-879979-10-1

__ __   copies of **Mindscapes & Mindsets** ($5.00)
ISBN 978-1-879979-08-X

__ __   copies of **Gardening: A Window on Our Soul** ($21.95)
ISBN 978-1-879979-05-5

Postage and handling per single copy: $ 3.00
Query postage costs if ordering multiple copies.

Order by check or invoice to:
Lifescape Enterprises
P. O. Box 218
West Mystic, CT 06388

Queries to:
Phone (860) 536-7179   fax (860) 536-2288
email: kathleenobeirne@aol.com

Credit card purchases:
To use your credit card, contact your local book store or
Bank Square Books Ltd (860) 536-3795
49 W. Main St., Mystic, CT 06355
Banksquarebks@msn.com

Re-order Information

___ ___ copies of **Mobile Student Passport** ($6.00)
ISBN 978-1-879979-06-3

___ ___ copies of **Life Is a Beach: Musings from the Sea** ($14.95)
ISBN 978-1-879979-09-8

___ ___ copies of **Birds of a Feather: Lessons from the Sea** ($19.95)
ISBN 978-1-879979-02-0

___ ___ copies of **Birds of a Feather: Behavior Patterns Matrix (**$5.00)
ISBN 978-1-879979-03-9

___ ___ copies of **Birds of a Feather: Educator's Guide** ($5.00)
ISBN 978-1-879979-11-X

___ ___ copies of **Birds of a Feather: Parent's Guide** ($5.00)
ISBN 978-1-879979-10-1

___ ___ copies of **Mindscapes & Mindsets** ($5.00)
ISBN 978-1-879979-08-X

___ ___ copies of **Gardening: A Window on Our Soul** ($21.95)
ISBN 978-1-879979-05-5

Postage and handling per single copy: $ 3.00
Query postage costs if ordering multiple copies.

Order by check or invoice to:
Lifescape Enterprises
P. O. Box 218
West Mystic, CT 06388

Queries to:
Phone (860) 536-7179   fax (860) 536-2288
mail: kathleenobeirne@aol.com

Credit card purchases:
To use your credit card, contact your local book store or
Bank Square Books Ltd (860) 536-3795
49 W. Main St., Mystic, CT 06355
Banksquarebks@msn.com